Boxing Referee

by
Zeke Crandall

This book is published by Zeke Crandall LLC., 6210 West Shaw Butte Drive, Glendale, 85304

The ISBN number is 978-0-9773784-8-7
the book's copyright number through the United States Library of Congress has been submitted.

Soft bound signed copies of the Simple Man are available for sale at discounted internet pricing on our website, www.arizonatales.com or by email, my email address is zekecrandall46@hotmail.com.

Other books from this author can be found on the authors website, www.arizonatales.com as well as online. All books are signed by the author. The author can also be reached on cell phone number 602 399-1811

The cover picture of Wyatt Earp was found in our National Archives and is public domain. The back cover drawing of the inside of Mechanics Pavilion appeared in the San Francisco Call Newspaper a few days before the fight.

Thank you,
Zeke Crandall

Preface

The more I do research on Wyatt Earp, the more fascinated I am with him and the more respect I have for this amazing man. Wyatt Earp was involved in so many firsts, that it is hard to believe that one man could have experienced so many in one lifetime. He spent his life on the line between legal and illegal and would bend the rules everyday of his life but from my research Wyatt Earp never did anything illegal.

Young Wyatt was drunk for three days after the death of his first wife Urilla, who died from Smallpox, and in his drunken state of mind and body, he asked for help from a stranger, who turned him down. So, Wyatt pistol whipped the man, stole the man's wallet, his horse and fled. He was caught, arrested and bound over for trial at a nearby town when a passer by recognized the stolen horse by its brand. Knowing his son was facing the death penalty, Nicholas Earp posted a bond that got his son out of jail. His father told him to head west and never look back or come back to Iowa, because if he did, there would be a hangman's noose waiting for him. From that day forward for the rest of his life, Wyatt Earp never took another alcoholic drink, which is why he always drank coffee.

He loved his second wife, Josie Marcus Earp and they were married for 48 years until his death in 1929 at the age of 81. Josie was a reformed prostitute, who worked as a stage hand for a traveling acting troop, when Earp met here in Tombstone in 1880. Josie suffered from a gambling addiction, a disease that forced her and her husband to travel a lot, always looking to strike it

2

rich in one way or another. She and her sister were heir's to a small fortune upon the death of their parents, who were owners of a bakery in San Francisco, their parents set up in a trust fund that allowed them enough monthly income to survive but not enough to not work for a living. They had a lot of adventures together, to say the least. From gold mining to running saloons, they always kept their eyes focused on the next big strike.

Wyatt was 16 years older than Josie when they were married, she was nineteen years old and Wyatt was 35. They both loved excitement and that was the glue that held them together. Josie was not able to have children. It is no wonder why after the life Wyatt lived as a lawman in Dodge City and Tombstone that Wyatt and Josie craved excitement. Not only was Wyatt Earp a great lawman and amazing faro dealer, he was also a polished boxer and referee of many professional bare knuckle fights in towns that he served as a lawman

One of the strangest boxing matches in the history of professional boxing took place at Mechanics Pavilion in San Francisco, California on the night of December 2, 1896.

Fifteen thousand fight fans crowded in the huge hall, occupying all available seats and flooding the aisles while a thirty-two piece band belted out *"Sweet Rosie O'Grady,"* the song that had become the mainstay at all boxing matches, probably due to the fact that most professional boxers of the time were of Irish decent.

Some of the men in the crowd, who couldn't find seats, climbed to the rafters and hung on precariously in order to get a better view of the up-coming heavyweight championship boxing match. The sportswriters were seated in a box high above the floor instead of their usual place at ringside. More than five thousand disgruntled ticket seekers were turned away from the box office. Most of them milled around outside until police were forced to clear the street for traffic.

The stage was set for one of the strangest championship fights in boxing history and none other than Wyatt Earp, as referee, again was involved in what was to be one of the first major controversial decisions in boxing history.

Bob Fitzsimmons — Wyatt Earp — Tom Sharkey

The picture of Wyatt Earp that is the cover of this book was taken when he was in his middle thirty years of age. This picture of Wyatt Earp is public domain and is widely available in postcard format and many other sources. Wyatt Earp was 47 years old at the time he refereed the boxing match between Fitzsimmons and Sharkey in 1896.

Chapter One

The world heavyweight championship fight was heavily advertised and promoted. The local and national newspapers carried the pre-fight festivities and hype, with articles written almost daily for thirty days up to fight night. The many articles written indicated, the match promised to be the fight of the year. The gamblers had been giving odds of three to one on the Champion "Fighting" Bob Fitzsimmons to win over the unranked contender, "Sailor" Tom Sharkey in Fitzsimmons first defense of his championship belt after being awarded the belt when Jim Corbett resigned.

Betting had shifted sharply by mid-afternoon on Wednesday December 2, 1896, the day of the fight, but few seemed to take notice. Everyone was too interested in the fight itself. Fitzsimmons had been the fastest rising heavyweight and number one contender when Corbett resigned and became Heavyweight Champion. Sharkey was the comer, who had beaten the prior Heavyweight Champion *"Gentleman Jim"* Corbett all of the ring for four rounds until the police arrived and stopped the fight, saving Corbett's butt from being beaten by a man they called in the papers, a nobody. *"Fighting Bob"* Fitzsimmons was noted for his boxing skills and hand speed, controlling the ring, and for being a clean fighter.

"Sailor" Tom Sharkey was a plodding slugger, who was very popular on the west coast. Both men were contenders in the heavyweight division and were both looking eagerly, toward a possible title match with prior Heavyweight Champion *"Gentleman Jim"* Corbett who was already making a comeback. For months the San Francisco fight

crowds were anxiously awaiting the big event.

Built in 1882, Mechanics' Pavilion was a large barn-like structure that stood in the downtown San Francisco Civic Center at the corner of Grove and Larkin streets. With a seating capacity of nearly 15,000, the building was originally set up for concerts, political conventions, circuses, and religious assemblies, but within a few years, it became best known for holding major prizefights. John L Sullivan, became the first of several world champions to fight in Mechanics Pavilion. The Mechanics Pavilion also staged a number of exhibition bouts, in point of fact Champion John L. Sullivan knocked out Paddy Ryan in three rounds of a scheduled twenty-five round World Heavyweight Championship bout ten years earlier in the year 1886 to retain his World Championship Belt.

Below is a photo of Mechanics' Pavilion, the building on the left side of this as it looked at the time of the fight in 1896, before it was destroyed in the earthquake in 1906. This photo was found in a San Francisco Chamber of Commerce tourist brochure.

On April 16, 1887, the State of New York banned professional prizefights, making San

6

Francisco the epicenter of boxing for the next decade. James Jeffries, the Heavyweight Champion of World in 1896, defended his title four times in San Francisco, all four bouts took place at Mechanics' Pavilion. Jim Jeffries defense of his crown against James Corbett, took place on August 14th 1903, that became the most financially successful fight in San Francisco history up to that time, as 10,600 patrons paid over $60,000 to watch Jeffries defeat *"Gentleman Jim"* in ten rounds.

The drawing below is how the inside of Mechanics Pavilion looked at the time of the fight. This drawing was found in our National Archives. It is set up for a concert. For a fight the ring would have been in the middle of the floor.

It was 5:12 on the morning of April 18, 1906, when San Francisco was hit with a 7.9 magnitude earthquake. Although Mechanics' Pavilion survived the impact, but nearby Central Emergency Hospital was not as lucky, most of it was turned into instant rubble. By 5:30 that morning, patients from the hospital, along with people injured in the quake were brought into Mechanics Pavilion, whose doors had been forced open. By mid-morning, Mechanics' Pavilion had become both hospital and morgue, as beds from neighboring hotels were being brought in by the hour. Unfortunately, by 1 pm, flames from the Hayes Valley fire reached the roof of Mechanics' Pavilion, and chief surgeon Dr Charles Miller ordered the building evacuated. Within hours, Mechanics' Pavilion was gone.

The following two newspaper article's appeared in the Sporting Section of the Detroit Evening News on Wednesday December 2, 1896. The author has a copy of the original paper in his rare newspaper collection. It was purchased from Timothy Hughes Rare Newspapers along with many more amazing original newspaper stories and articles. Timothy Hughes specializes on collecting famous news articles. Below is the first article and the second article follows. Both articles were on the same page of the same edition;

ALL "FITZ"

He must whip Corbett through Sharkey by stopping the Sailor in short order.

Joseph Donovan, the well-known fistic correspondent, in the Chicago News sums up Sharkey's chances in the big fight at San Francisco tonight as follows;

"In meeting Sharkey said of Fitzsimmons, that he is going to try to lay out a man whom both Choynski and Jim Corbett failed to squelch, and a man who has been bragging considerably

since, that he had Jim Corbett in his power after four rounds of rough mixture. Fitz, of course, will strive for a rapid knock-out."

Something like the Corbett-Sharkey go repeated in this; for in that Jim sailed in immediately at tap of the first gong to put the sailor out. He was solicitous to show his fellow townsmen that he could thump the sailor to better effect in four rounds than Choynski could do in eight. Now steps Fitz in along the same lines; he has ten rounds to do Corbett vicariously through the toughened tar, but he will make a mighty effort to stretch his opponent's body on the slabs in

four rounds or less.

"It is difficult to see anybody in it but Fitz. Certainly the Kangaroo has proved himself the cleanest knock-out hitter in the ring and no man of Sharkey's limited experience should hope to stand him off along that line. It has been reported that Sharkey thinks Fitz can't thump hard enough to knock him out, but here Tommy will find himself wrong."

Below is the second article pertaining to the fight that was to take place later that evening in San Francisco, and again appeared on the front page of the sports page with the article above.

IT'S A CINCH

That's what "Fitz" thinks he has to do in his battle with Sharkey tonight. The Sailor also, is confident of

9

*victory. **Nearly 14,000 seats have been sold in advance of the fight.***

San Francisco, Dec. 2- Both Fitzsimmons and Sharkey have ceased training and are ready for their meeting in the arena of the National Athletic Club tonight. When Fitz was weighed yesterday morning in his fighting togs for the last time, he tipped the scales at exactly 173 ¼ pounds and this will be about his weight when he goes into the ring around ten o'clock this evening. He has never stripped as heavy in any battle he has ever fought, but the added flesh is as hard as nails. His trainers think the affair will last about three rounds and that Fitz will put Sharkey out with a straight punch.

"Like all of my battles this is going to be a short, quick go," said Fitz. "I suppose Sharkey will play endurance, but even if he were able to keep away from me, which he cannot, I can stand the endurance part of it as long as he can. It's a cinch and I never though it was anything else from the day the match was made."

Ring experts express the opinion that Sharkey is almost in too fine condition, but they say owing to his youth and sound constitution, the rest he will get today will counteract any weakness his seven weeks' exercise might have entailed. The sailor is also confident of victory. He believes he will win inside of seven rounds and said he was going to put up a fight that would surprise "all."

"I can hit just as hard as Fitzsimmons can, was the way he put it, and he will know before the fun is over that he has been in a fight.

As yet he has not seen Fitzsimmons and what he knows
of the Australian is second-hand knowledge. He is only interested in reports he has heard of Fitzsimmons' heavy right hand jabs, and it may have been just pure chance o n his part, but the sailor has developed his left arm hitting power punches.

HOW THE BETTING RANGES

Sharkey is the popular West Coast favorite, while Fitz is the choice of the crowd conclusively proven at the pool rooms around town last night, for Sharkey, betting money was never lacking when Fitzsimmons cash was announced. So strong were the sailor's backers that Sharkey would be put out in six rounds to nine and ten that he would stay in the fight even that long. Small amounts of money were placed on Fitz at ten to four and twenty-five to ten, but the betting settled at twenty to nine to one. Big money went into the betting pools at this figure.

The seating arrangements are as nearly perfect as the capacity of the pavilion will permit. The ring situated in the center of the building. Over 12K of the 14K thousand seats have been sold as of this morning.

Chapter Two

At exactly 10:09 o'clock Wednesday evening on December 2, 1896, Bob Fitzsimmons made his way down a crowded aisle and climbed into the ring, followed by his manager, Martin Julian, and his seconds, Dan Hickey and Jack Stelzner. The buzz of the large crowd followed him all the way and burst into a crescendo of cheers as he climbed through the ropes and into the ring. Fitzsimmons was self-confident, unconcerned and smiling as he acknowledged the roars of approval from the crowd, as he walked to the edge of the ring and stood talking with Major Frank McLaughlin, who was the organizer of the boxing match, before taking off his robe and moving around the ring shadow boxing with every move.

Robert James "Bob" Fitzsimmons (May 26, 1863 – October 22, 1917). Fitzsimmons was an English professional boxer, also of Irish decent, who made boxing history as the sport's first three-division world championships. He also achieved fame for beating Gentleman Jim Corbett, the man who beat John L. Sullivan and is in The Guinness Book of World Records as the lightest Heavyweight Champion in the history of the sport.

Nicknamed *"Ruby Robert"* and *"The Freckled Wonder,"* Fitzsimmons took pride in his lack of scars and appeared in the ring wearing heavy woolens underwear to conceal the disparity between his trunk and under developed lower body and legs. He was also known for his pure fighting skills due to dislike of training for fights, which would ultimately cost him at times in his career. Bob Fitzsimmons was ranked as #8 on the list of 100 of the greatest boxer's of all time by Ring Magazine.

Bob Fitzsimmons was the youngest of 12 children. He was born in Helston, Cornwall, England. His father was James Fitzsimmons, born in County Armagh, Ireland and his mother was Jane Strongman, born in St. Clement, Cornwall, England; making Fitzsimmons half Irish and half English by blood.

The Fitzsimmons family immigrated to New Zealand when Bob was nine years of age, along with his parents, brothers and sisters. His family settled in the town of Timaru, New Zealand, among many other English settlers. Bob became a blacksmith in his older brother Jarrett's blacksmith shop and livery stable.

Between 1880 and 1881, Bob Fitzsimmons reigned as champion of the Jen Mace Tournament in New Zealand. Some boxing historians say, he officially began his career as a professional boxer in New Zealand later in 1881. Fitzsimmons knocked out Herbert Slade in two rounds in his first fight. Fitzsimmons went on to have six amateur fights in New Zealand, two of them were bare knuckle events and in the other two, four ounce gloves were used. Fitzsimmons won one and lost five. Obviously, Bob Fitzsimmons had a very inauspicious start to his boxing career.

Boxing record books show Fitzsimmons officially began his professional boxing career in 1883, in Australia. He beat Jim Crawford by knocking out his opponent in the third round of their scheduled 25 round bare knuckle fight. Fitzsimmons had his first 28 definitive professional fights in Australia, where he lost the Australian Middleweight title to Mick Dooley *(rumors circled of a fixed bout)* and where he also won a fight by knockout, while on the floor, when Edward Starlight Robins dropped

13

Fitzsimmons to the canvas in round nine of their fight, he also broke his hand and could not continue, therefore the referee declared Fitzsimmons the winner by a knockout.

By this point in his career, Fitzsimmons had established his own style. He developed a certain movement and caginess from one of the great bare-knuckle fighter's, Jen Mace. Mace had encouraged Bob to develop his punching technique and he revolutionized this, drawing on the enormous forearm power he possessed that he gained from working as a blacksmith. Fitzsimmons delivered short, accurate, straight and usually conclusive punches. He soon built up a reputation as by far the hardest puncher in professional boxing.

Moving on to the United States, Fitzsimmons fought four more times in 1890, winning three and fought to a draw in the fourth match. Then, on January 14, 1891, in New Orleans, Louisiana, Fitzsimmons won his first world title from Jack Nonpareil Dempsey. Fitzsimmons knocked out Dempsey *(from whom the later Jack Dempsey would take his name)* in the thirteenth round of their scheduled twenty-five round bout to become the World Middleweight Champion. Fitzsimmons knocked Dempsey down at least thirteen times and by the finish left him in such a pitiable condition that he begged him to quit. Since Dempsey would not do so, Fitzsimmons knocked him out and then carried him to his corner. On July 22, 1891, police broke up his fight with Jim Hall in New York, prize fights were illegal at that time in the NY, after Fitzsimmons had knocked Hall down several times.

Fitzsimmons spent the next two years fighting non-title bouts and exhibitions until giving Hall a chance at the title in 1893. He retained the crown by a knocking out Jim Hall in round four of a twenty five round scheduled bare knuckle boxing match. Fighting Bob Fitzsimmons spent the rest of that year doing exhibitions, and on June 2, 1893, he had scheduled a two-way exhibition where he would demonstrate in public how to hit the boxing bag and then how to box against a real opponent. Reportedly, two freak accidents happened that day: Fitzsimmons hit the bag so hard that it broke, and then his opponent of that day allegedly slipped, getting hit in the head and the boxing exhibition was cancelled

After vacating his Middleweight Championship title, Fitzsimmons began campaigning among heavyweight division as the light heavyweight division did not exist at that time.

In 1896, Fitzsimmons won a disputed version of the World Heavyweight Championship in a fight in Langtry, Texas, against the Irish native fighter Peter Maher. On March 17, 1897, in Carson City, Nevada, Fitzsimmons knocked out San Francisco, California native "Gentleman" Jim Corbett, generally recognized as the legitimate World Heavyweight Champion *(having won the title from John L. Sullivan in 1892)* in round 14 of their scheduled twenty-five round bout. This constituted a remarkable achievement, as Jim Corbett, a skilled boxer, weighed fourteen pounds more than Fitzsimmons. He out-boxed Fitzsimmons for several rounds, knocked him down in the sixth round and badly damaged his face with his jab, left hook and right hand, but Fitzsimmons kept coming and Corbett began to tire. In the 14th round, Fitzsimmons won the title with his incredibly strong and powerful *"solar plexus"* body punch. Corbett collapsed in agony. Fitzsimmons' solar plexus body

15

punch became legendary, although he himself may never have used the phrase. The entire fight was filmed by Enoch J. Rector and released to cinemas as *"The Corbett-Fitzsimmons Fight,"* the longest film ever released at the time. Using her maiden name, it was covered by Nellie Verrill Mighels Davis, the first woman to report a prize fight for a national newspaper. She was a reporter for the Carson City Nevada Appeal Newspaper, where after her husband died when she was just 35 years old, became the editor of the Appeal Newspaper. Fitzsimmons spent the rest of 1897 speaking to reporters, who published everything he did from taking a bath to drinking a beer with politicians.

In 1899, Fitzsimmons and James J. Jeffries succeeded in boxing in New York City for the Heavyweight World Championship title without the police intervening to stop the match, so the match most probably took place at an underground club. Most people gave Jeffries little chance, even though at 6'2" tall and weighing 225 pounds, massively outweighed Fitzsimmons, who was 5'11" tall and weighed 185 pounds, and was far younger than Fighting Bob. With an eleventh round knockout, of Fitzsimmons, Jeffries became the World Heavyweight Champion.

In June 1901 Fitzsimmons took part in a wrestling match against top ten Heavyweight contender Gus Ruhlin. Fitzsimmons lost and went back to boxing. He then enjoyed legitimate boxing knockouts of both Ruhlin and Sharkey on his comeback trail from losing the title to Jeffries.

In 1902, Fitzsimmons and Jeffries had a rematch, once again with the World Heavyweight Championship at stake. Fitzsimmons battered Jeffries, who suffered horrible punishment. With his nose and cheek bones broken, most would have sympathized with Jeffries had he quit, but he kept going until his enormous weight advantage and youth took over and Bob Fitzsimmons suffered another knockout at the hands of Jim Jeffries in round eight.

September 1903 proved a tragic month for Fitzsimmons, as his rival, Con Coughlin, died the day after suffering a one-round knockout at the hands of Bob Fitzsimmons. But less than two months later, Fitzsimmons made history by defeating World Light Heavyweight Champion George Gardiner by a decision in 20 rounds, thus becoming the first boxer to win titles in three weight-divisions, middleweight, heavyweight and the new, light heavyweight division.

Soon afterward, he went back to the heavyweight division, because the heavyweight division was the only division where the big money existed, where he kept fighting until 1914, with mixed results. He boxed Jack Johnson, and film historians believe that his fight with Bob Sweeney became the first boxing-fight captured on film.

Although Fitzsimmons became a world champion in each of the Middleweight, Light Heavyweight and Heavyweight divisions, historians do not consider him the first world Light Heavyweight Champion to become World Heavyweight Champion, because he won the Heavyweight title before winning the Light Heavyweight belt.

Michael Spinks counts as the first Light Heavyweight World Champion to win the Heavyweight belt as well. However, Fitzsimmons was the first Middleweight Champion to win the Heavyweight title and the only Heavyweight Champion to drop down and win the Light

Heavyweight title.

In 2003, Roy Jones Jr. joined Fitzsimmons, Michael Moorer and Spinks as the only men to have won world championships at both light heavyweight and heavyweight.

Fitzsimmons's exact record remains unknown, as the boxing world often kept records poorly during his era, but Fitzsimmons swears that he had more than 350 fights, *(that could have involved exaggeration on his part but for sure he also would have included amateur fights)*

Bob Fitzsimmons died in Chicago, Illinois of pneumonia at the age of 54 in 1917, survived by his fourth wife. His grave lies in the Graceland Cemetery, Chicago. Having four wives, a gambling habit and a susceptibility to confidence tricksters, he did not hold on to the money he made.

The International Boxing Hall of Fame has made Bob Fitzsimmons a member in its *"Old Timer"* category. In 2003 Ring Magazine named Fitzsimmons number eight of all time among Professional Boxing's' best punchers

The photos below of Bob Fitzsimmons found in our National Archives.

Robert James "Bob" Fitzsimmons aka; Ruby and Fighting Bob Fitzsimmons. Bob Fitzsimmons was born in Helston, Cornwall, United Kingdom on May 26, 1863. His faith was Angelican Catholic. He died on October 22, 1917, at the age of 54 in Chicago Illinois. His hometown was Timaru, New Zealand. Fitzsimmons was 5'11 ½" tall and weighed 195 pounds. He had a 71 ½ inch reach. His professional record according to Ring Magazine was 66 wins (59 by way of knockout), 7 losses and 5 Draws.

Below is a picture taken at ringside of the Fitzsimmons-Corbett Championship fight on May 22, 1897. This photo was found in our National Archives. Fitz is on the left, Corbett pictured on the right.

Chapter Three

Tom Sharkey entered the ring about four minutes after Fitzsimmons entered the ring. Again through cheers of the crowd, as he walked down the aisle to the ring, walking with him were, Danny Lynch, his manager, along with his trainer Danny Needham, and seconds Billy Smith and George Allen. After entering the ring Sharkey went right over to Fitzsimmons and they shook hands.

Tom "Sailor" Sharkey (November 26, 1873–April 17, 1953) was a boxer who fought two fights with heavyweight champion James J. Jeffries in the heavyweight division before entering the ring against Fitzsimmons that evening. Sharkey's recorded ring career spanned from 1893 to 1904. He is credited with having won 40 fights, winning 37 by way of knockout, 7 losses, and 5 draws. Sharkey was named to the Ring Magazine's list of 100 greatest boxers of all time.

Sharkey was born in Dundalk, Ireland. His story began when he ran away from home and went to sea as a cabin boy. In 1892, Sharkey landed in New York City and joined the United States Navy. He was eventually deployed to Hawaii where he began his pro fighting career.

Sharkey started out in Hawaii knocking out any competitor, who entered the ring to fight him. In 1894 he moved to California and there he recorded fourteen straight fights, winning all fourteen by way of knockout. For the most part his competitors were mostly mediocre opponents and inside two years added five more, one over the tough veteran, Billy Smith, the Australian Heavyweight Champion

Sharkey had a fine apartment on Fourteenth Street, in downtown New York City. His floor was paved with silver dollars. When he entered the ring to fight John L. Sullivan, he swore that one-half of the money he won would be used to pave the floor of his home. It was a terrific fight, and it went to a draw, with the result that Tom's share of the purse was sufficient to enable him to carry out his resolution; and Sharkey's floor is still one of the sights in New York to this day.

Tom Sharkey was a crude brawler from the *"Old School."* At the sound of the opening bell, he attacked his opponent, throwing bombs until the end. He was a rough and durable violator of rules. To Sharkey, the rules were simply restrictions that kept a real fight from taking place

Standing 5 ft 8 in tall and weighing 205 pounds, Sharkey was a standup brawler, who came right after his opponents. Sharkey was easy to hit, but rough and tumble along with throwing a heavy punch *(A boxing term for a hard puncher).* He had unusually broad shoulders for a man of his height, and sported a tattoo of a star and battleship on his chest. In 1900 he also acquired a large cauliflower ear, courtesy of a brawl with Gus Ruhlin that added to his persona.

On December 2, 1896 Sharkey fought a controversial battle with future heavyweight champion Bob Fitzsimmons. The bout had been billed for the heavyweight championship of the world, as it was thought that the champion, James J. Corbett, aka Gentleman Jim, had relinquished the crown. But in point of fact Corbett just took a short leave of absence from the ring and then resumed his fighting career a few months later. He continued to be recognized as the Heavyweight Champion of the World, until he was knocked out by Bob Fitzsimmons in a title bout on May 22, 1897.

The film of this fight no longer exists in its entirety; however, it is known from contemporary sources that the film included all fourteen rounds of the event, each round lasting three minutes. This was not unusual for a boxing film, although each round would previously have been presented as a separate attraction. What made this film exceptional is a five-minute introduction that showed former champion John L. Sullivan *(whom Corbett defeated in 1892)* and his manager, Billy Madden, introducing the event, the introduction of referee George Siler, and both boxers entering the ring in their robes.

The film also caught the one-minute rest between each round and, when the film was reissued in Boston and many of its subsequent reissues, including in Dublin, included a ten-minute epilogue of the empty ring at the end of the fight, into which members of the audience eventually stormed. Even with these approximate timings, the film ran a minimum of 71 minutes, and sources generally report that it exceeded 90 or 100 minutes. The film climaxes with Fitzsimmons hitting Corbett in the solar plexus for a knockout, Corbett crawling outside the space of the camera so that he is not visible above the waist.

In '98, after a tune-up fight with Sailor Brown, Sharkey was matched with 28-year-old Joe Choynski, a clever boxer, who had not suffered a loss since 1891. It proved to be a terrible mismatch as Choynski dominated the action from the opening bell, attacking the stocky sailor without mercy. But try as he might, the battle-wise San Franciscan could not stop Tom Sharkey. At one point he managed to drive him through the ropes with a flurry of blows, but the Irishman merely clenched his teeth and climbed back in the ring. When he could plod in close to the taller man, Sharkey would wail away at his lean mid-section with savage lefts and rights, but Choynski would push away and smash him at long range. Joe hit him with every ounce of strength he possessed, and it was considerable, but Sharkey would not yield. Finally, the bell sounded and the bout was awarded to the bloody ex-seaman as per contract.

Sharkey was involved in another controversial fight when he faced Corbett on November 22, 1898. In this bout Sharkey manhandled the shifty and elusive Corbett. He threw him to the ground, hit him with hard punches to the body and head and seemed on the verge of imminent victory when one of Corbett's seconds jumped into the ring in the ninth round. The referee promptly disqualified Corbett and awarded the bout to Sharkey.

A draw with fellow Irishman Peter Maher, in New York, four quick knockouts in Britain and a six-round stoppage of the Barrier Champion, Joe Goddard, put him near the top of the heap and set up a rematch with Joe Choynski, who had been aching for a chance to remove a blot from his reputation. The match proved nothing, ending in a draw. Again the hard-punching Californian had been unable to administer a finishing stroke, and this time he had taken as much as he had dished out. It was Sharkey's 34th bout without a loss, and only one man stood in his way. Jim Jeffries!

On May 6, 1898 Sharkey finally had his match with James J. Jeffries. They fought twenty rounds in San Francisco with Jim Jeffries firmly established Tom Sharkey's reputation as an iron man. Outweighed by more than twenty pounds, he took the fight to the boilermaker in the early going and even managed to bull Jeffries around the ring. For sixty minutes, broken at intervals of three minutes, Tom Sharkey and Jim Jeffries fought toe-to-toe at ring center. It was a battle of attrition; two great iron-clad warships hurling explosive shells at each other without thought of surrender. Through the last few rounds the tide turned in Jeffries favor as he landed again and again with murderous left hooks and right uppercuts to the smaller man's rock-like head. The remaining seconds expired with both men in a state of complete physical and mental exhaustion. When the referee called the two battlers to his side, it was big Jim Jefferies thick right arm that was raised in victory amidst cries of protest from Sharkey's supporters.

Tom was more determined than ever to win the heavyweight title; especially when he saw Jeffries go on to win the crown from his old foe, Bob Fitzsimmons. So he set about establishing himself as the number one contender, stopping big Gus Ruhlin in one round, winning against Jim Corbett, and knocking out wily Kid McCoy and Jack McCormick. But all of his efforts were to prove futile. Jeffries still stood in his way.

The two fought a memorable twenty-five round rematch bout on November 3, 1899 in Coney Island, New York. The match was the first championship fight filmed for motion pictures, and the lights required for the filming were so hot that they burned the hair from the top of both fighters' heads. The last round of the fight was not recorded, however, because the camera operator ran out of film.

The fight was a ring classic. Sharkey took the early lead when he battered the larger Jeffries during the early stages of the bout. Jeffries, however, Jeffries was very powerful and gained control of the fight in the later rounds. Both fighters, despite suffering severe injuries during the bout went all out in the final round, which most in attendance believed was won by Jeffries. In any event the bout was awarded to Jeffries, although many felt Sharkey had won. During this fight the indomitable Sharkey suffered a broken nose and two broken ribs, and his left ear swelled to the size of a grapefruit. After this fight Jeffries and Sharkey became friends. Jim Jeffries always considered his second battle with Tom Sharkey the hardest fight of his entire career. It went a full twenty-five rounds, in near unbearable heat, that melted fifteen pounds or more off each of them, and it ended once again with Jeff's arm raised. Sharkey, his entire face covered with blood, his jaw broken and several ribs shattered, was helped into a waiting ambulance and rushed to the hospital.

Although he survived the beating, Tom was just about through as a fighter. On his next fight Tom managed to KO Joe Goddard again and finally won clearly against Choynski, by a KO in the second round of their scheduled twenty round fight, but the year ended in disaster with losses to Ruhlin and again to Fitzsimmons.

For all intents and purposes Sharkey's career came to a halt on June 25, 1902 when Gus Ruhlin, on the comeback trail since losing to Jeffries the previous year, performed a workmanlike demolition job on Sharkey in a London, England ring, knocking him out in the initial seconds of the eleventh round. Sharkey retired for good in 1904, after a six-round draw with Canada's Champion Jack Munroe.

Although he never won a championship his friendship with Jim Jeffries lasted well after both of their boxing careers ended. Sharkey toured with Jeffries doing vaudeville acts until Tom came down with what was thought to be a simple lung infection in the winter of 1938.

In late December of 1938 Tom "Sailor" Sharkey entered Laguna Honda Hospital in San Francisco, according to newspaper accounts, desperately ill. He was diagnosed with Tuberculosis. After a fifteen year battle from the disease he died there 1953 and is buried at Golden Gate National Cemetery in San Bruno, California.

Tom "Sailor" Sharkey was born in the town of Dundalk, Ireland on November 26, 1873. Sharkey was a full blood Irishman. He died at the age of 79 on April 4, 1953 in his hometown of San Francisco, California and was Irish Catholic. Sharkey stood 5'8" tall and weighed 190 pounds. He had a 70 ½ reach. His ring record was; 37 professional fights, he won 34 by way of knockout. He lost seven professional fights and he had seven draws. His total number of fights was 52 including 273 rounds. Below are photos of Tom "Sailor" Sharkey found in the Ring Magazine and many other readily available sources.

The photos below of Tom Sharkey were found in our National Archives

Chapter Four

Master of ceremonies, Billy Jordan was already in the ring by the time both Sharkey and Fitzsimmons were there in the ring warming up for the upcoming match on that Wednesday evening, December 2. 1896. Jordan handed a package containing the gloves to Police Captain Whitman, who opened the package and inspected the 6 ounce gloves to make sure they met the specifications. Then he tossed a pair to each corner's manager. At that point the gloves were put on both fighters as they continued to bounce around the ring shadow boxing as they readied themselves for the fight.

At 10:16 pm the fighters were introduced to the crowd by Billy Jordan, while Martin Julian and Needham stood alongside the ring talking about the referee, who had been chosen by both managers. Billy Jordan walked to the ropes and, raising his hands for silence, called out the name;

"Wyatt Earp! Wyatt Earp!"

You heard right one of the crowd was heard to say loudly. It's him all right, the same Wyatt Earp, who was the famous Dodge City and Tombstone lawman. At that point a neatly dressed man of good proportions and a drooping handlebar mustache arouse from a seat near the ring and strolled toward the ring. Earp's name may have meant nothing to some in the crowd, but to most of the sporting men present, he was well known. He had been moving in sporting circles for many years. As he walked toward the ring the crowd noticed Captain Whitman call Lynch and Julian together. Those near the ring sensed there was some disagreement about Earp as the referee. A word was whispered to Jordan

Master of ceremonies Billy Jordan turned to the crowd and spoke;

> *"Gentlemen; Mr. Wyatt Earp has been selected to be the referee of this boxing match. But owing to rumors going around that there is something crooked about Mr. Earp, that Mr. Julian has heard, he refused to accept Mr. Earp as a qualified referee."*

The announcement was met with boos and yells of displeasure by the crowd. Wyatt Earp stood by the ring expressionless. He definitely was used to displeasure attached to his name as the referee as well as everywhere else in his life. Billy Julian now spoke for himself;

> *"I want to announce that Mr. Sharkey's manager, the club officials, and myself met and tried to select a referee. I named a half dozen men qualified to be the referee, among who was Hiram Cook and several others. Mr. Lynch objected to all of them. The National Athletic Club then selected Wyatt Earp, who in point of fact turned down the job, until he was talked into being the referee for this bout."*

Someone in the crowed confirmed the selection;

> *"Wyatt Earp is a good man and a great referee!"*

Cheers of approval bellowed out everywhere in the crowd. Martin Julian then spoke;

28

"When we first heard that Mr. Wyatt Earp had been selected, he was a satisfactory choice to us, but since 6:30 this evening several San Francisco sporting men have come to us and related that the fight was fixed and the referee was involved in the fix."

Someone in the crowd shouted loudly so all could hear;

"Name them."

Tom Sharkey's manager took the floor and spoke;

"Gentlemen, Mr. Fitzsimmons and his representative's along with myself met with the officers of the club, as well as, Mr. Sharkey and his men have lived up to every article, including the selection of Mr. Wyatt Earp. He has agreed to, and both men are ready and willing to fight with the referee selected by the club."

The crowd went wild with shouts of approval. Master of Ceremonies, Billy Jordan raised his hands for silence once more and spoke loudly;

"Again I say, Mr. Julian is willing to accept any referee in the house."

Jordan then again raised his hands and signaled for quiet;

"Wyatt Earp! Wyatt Earp! The crowd shouted from every section in the pavilion."

29

At this point J.D. Gibbs, representative of the National Athletic Club climbed into the ring. After a brief council, Jordan turned to the crowd and spoke;

> *"Mr. Julian will accept Hiram Cook or any other good referee."*

At that point a call was made for referee Hiram Cook. When he failed to appear the hooting and hollering commenced again.

Bob Fitzsimmons, who had been sitting in his corner listening to all of the commotion rose from his seat and signaled to Billy Jordan that he wished to speak;

> *"I have given it all in every one of my fights and I will give it all tonight in this fight but there is only one thing I ask and that is Mr. Wyatt Earp needs to take off those bandages on his hands, neither me or Tom have none on our hands, so its only right that he removes them from his hands."*

As Wyatt removed the bandages from his hands the crowd shouted with cheers of approval. Billy Jordan after raising his arms to silence the crowd announced;

> *"Mr. Fitzsimmons and Mr. Sharkey accept Mr. Wyatt Earp for tonight's referee."*

Wyatt Earp passed up the opportunity to step down gracefully. Instead once he removed his bandages, he peeled off his coat and revealed, to his embarrassment, a holstered revolver. Police Captain Whitman, who was present, fined Mr. Earp fifty dollars for brandishing a pistol in a public place and made Earp take off the belt, holster and pistol, then the real action began.

The line drawing below appeared in the San Examiner newspaper the day after the fight and depicts Wyatt Earp surrendering his revolver to Police Captain Wittman before refereeing the Sharkey-Fitzsimmons fight on December 2, 1896. This copy is courtesy of the Bancroft Library.

Chapter Five

Over the next three chapters it is important to include a brief history of Wyatt Earp as he played a huge part in history again, as a referee of this World Heavyweight Championship Elimination Match.

Wyatt Berry Stapp Earp (March 19, 1848 – January 13, 1929) Wyatt Earp was born in Monmouth, Illinois, on March 19, 1848, to Nicholas Porter Earp and Virginia Ann Cooksey. From his father's first marriage, Wyatt had an elder half-brother, Newton, and a half-sister Mariah Ann, who died at the age of ten months. Earp had five brothers and four sisters, who were his blood family. Wyatt Earp was named after his father's commanding officer in the Mexican-American War, Captain Wyatt Berry Stapp, of the 2nd Company Illinois Mounted Volunteers. In March 1849, the Earp's left Monmouth for California but settled in Iowa. Their farm consisted of 160 acres Northeast of Pella, Iowa.

Wyatt Earp spent his early life in Iowa. His first wife Urilla Sutherland Earp died from Typhoid Fever, while pregnant less than a year after they married. Within the next two years he was arrested, sued twice, escaped from jail, then was arrested three more times for public intoxication as well as *"keeping and being found in a house of ill-fame."* Earp landed in the cattle boomtown of Wichita, Kansas where he became a deputy marshal for one year and developed a solid reputation as a lawman. In 1876 he followed his brother Virgil Earp to Dodge City, Kansas where he became a deputy town marshal. In the winter of 1878 he went to Texas chasing an outlaw by the name of Dave Rudabaugh where he met John Henry "Doc" Holliday whom Earp credited with saving his life on one occasion.

Continually drawn to boomtowns and opportunity, Earp left Dodge City in 1879, and with his brothers James and Virgil, moved to Tombstone, Arizona. The Earps bought an interest in the Vizina mine and some water rights. There, the Earp's clashed with a loose federation of outlaws called *"The Cowboys."* Wyatt, Virgil, and their younger brother Morgan held various law enforcement positions that put them in conflict with Tom and Frank McLaury, along with brothers Ike and Billy Clanton, who all threatened to kill the Earp's. The conflict escalated over the next year, culminating on October 26, 1881 in the Gunfight at the O.K. Corral, during which the Earp's and Holliday killed three of the Cowboys. In the next five months, Virgil was ambushed and maimed; losing his left arm and Morgan was assassinated. Wyatt, his brother Warren, Holliday, along with two friends and pursued the Cowboys they thought responsible.

After the death of the last man thought to be involved in the death of his brother, Johnny Ringo, the Earps left Tombstone. Wyatt Earp continually invested in various mining interests and saloons. He and his third wife, Josie Earp, *(Wyatt Earp was never married to Maddie Earp, but he considered her his second wife)*, in their later years, the couple moved between Los Angeles and the Mojave Desert, where the town of Earp, California and a town of the same name is in Arizona was named after him. Although his brother Virgil had far more experience as a lawman, Wyatt, who outlived Virgil, and was made famous by a largely fictionalized biography, Frontier Marshal, by Stuart Lake, that has been the subject of and model for a large number of films, TV shows, biographies and works of fiction. But it is true that, unlike his brothers and his ally Doc Holliday, who participated in several gun battles with him, Wyatt was never wounded during his entire lifetime, which only contributed to his mystique.

On March 4, 1856, Earp's father Nicholas sold his farm and returned to Turtle, Illinois, where he was elected the municipal constable, serving at this post for about three years. He was caught and convicted in 1859 for bootlegging. Nicholas was unable to pay the fines, and a lien was put against e Earp's farm property. It was sold at auction in November 1859, and the family left again for Pella, Iowa. After their move, Nicholas returned to Monmouth throughout 1860 to sell his other properties and resolve several lawsuits for debt and accusations of tax evasion.

During the family's second stay in Pella, the American Civil War began. Newton, James, and Virgil joined the Union Army on November 11, 1861. While his father was busy recruiting and drilling local companies, Wyatt, along with his two younger brothers, Morgan and Warren, were left in charge of tending 80-acre corn crop. Only 13 years old, Wyatt was too young to enlist, but he tried on several occasions to run away and join the army. Each time his father found him and brought him home. James was severely wounded in the battle at Fredericktown, Missouri, and returned home in the summer of 1863. Newton and Virgil fought several battles in the east and later returned home after the war. On May 12, 1864, the Earp family joined a wagon train heading to California.

By late summer 1865, Virgil found work as a driver for Phineas Banning's Stage Coach Line in California's Imperial Valley, and 16 year old Wyatt was his shotgun guard. In the spring of 1866, Wyatt Earp became a teamster, transporting cargo for Chris Taylor. His assigned trail in 1866 to 1868 was from Wilmington, through San Bernadino and Las Vegas, New Mexico to Salt Lake City, Utah Territory.

In the spring of 1868, Earp was hired by Charles Chrisman to transport supplies for the construction of the Union Pacific Railroad. He learned gambling and boxing while working on the railhead in Wyoming, and at the railroad town of Hell on Wheels young Wyatt Earp refereed his first boxing match between John Shanssey and Mike Donovan.

In the summer of 1868, the Earp family moved east again to Lamar, Missouri, where Wyatt's father Nicholas became the local constable. Wyatt rejoined the family the next year. When Nicholas resigned on November 17, 1869 as constable to become the justice of the peace, Wyatt was appointed constable in his place. On November 26, in return for his appointment, Earp filed a bond of $1,000. His sureties for this bond were his father, Nicholas Porter Earp; his paternal uncle, Jonathan Douglas Earp (April 28, 1824–October 10, 1900); and James Maupin.

In late 1869, Wyatt met Urilla Sutherland (1849–c.1870), the daughter of hotel-keeper William and Permelia Sutherland, formerly of New York City. They married in Lamar on January 10, 1870, and in August 1870 bought a lot on the outskirts of town for $50. Urilla was pregnant and about to deliver their first child when she died from Typhoid Fever later that year. In November, 1870 Wyatt sold the lot and a house on it for $75. He ran against his elder half-brother Newton for the office of constable, winning by 137 votes to 108.

Within two years of Urilla's death, Wyatt had a series of legal problems. On March 14, 1871, Barton County, Missouri filed a lawsuit against Earp and his sureties. He was in charge of collecting license fees for Lamar, which funded local schools. Earp was accused of failing to turn in the fees. On March 31, James Cromwell filed a lawsuit against Wyatt, alleging that Wyatt had falsified court documents about the amount of money Earp had collected from Cromwell to satisfy a judgment. To make up the difference between what Earp turned in and Cromwell actually owed the court seized Cromwell's mowing machine and sold it for $38. Cromwell's suit claimed Earp owed him $75, the estimated value of the machine.

On March 28, 1871 Wyatt, Edward Kennedy, and John Shown were charged with stealing two horses, "each of the value of one hundred dollars," from William Keys while in the Indian County. On April 6, Deputy United States Marshal J. G. Owens arrested Earp for the horse theft. Commissioner James Churchill arraigned Earp on April 14, and set bail at $500. On May 15, an indictment against Earp, Kennedy, and Shown was issued. Anna Shown, John Shown's wife, claimed that Earp and Kennedy got her husband drunk and then threatened his life to persuade him to help. On June 5 Edward Kennedy was acquitted while the case against Earp and John Shown remained. Earp didn't wait for the trial. He climbed out through the roof of his jail and headed for Peoria, Illinois.

Years afterward, Wyatt's biographer Stuart Lake reported that Wyatt took to hunting buffalo during the winter of 1871-72, but Earp was arrested three times in the Peoria area during that period. Earp is listed in the city directory for Peoria during 1872 as a resident in the house of Jane Haspel, who operated a brothel. In February 1872, Peoria police raided the brothel, arresting four women and three men: Wyatt Earp, Morgan Earp, and George Randall. Wyatt and the others were charged with *"Keeping and being found in a house of ill-fame."* They were later fined twenty dollars plus costs for the criminal infraction. He was arrested for the same crime in May 1872 and late September 1872. He was probably employed as an enforcer or bouncer. He may have hunted buffalo during 1873-74 before he went to Wichita.

Like Ellsworth, Wichita was a railroad terminal that was a destination for cattle drives from Texas. Such cattle boom towns on the frontier were raucous places filled with drunken, armed cowboys celebrating at the end of long drives. When the summer-time cattle drives ended and the cowboys left, Earp searched for something to do. In October 1874, he earned a bit of money helping an off-duty police officer find thieves who had stolen a man's wagon. He got his name in the paper. Earp officially joined the Wichita marshal's office on April 21, 1875, after the election of Mike Meagher as city marshal or police chief, making $100 per month. He also dealt faro at the Long Branch Saloon. In late 1875, the local paper (Wichita Beacon) published this story;

> *"On last Wednesday (December 8), policeman Earp found a stranger lying near the bridge in a drunken stupor. He took him to the 'cooler' and on searching him, found in the neighborhood of $500*

on his person. He was taken next morning, before his honor, the police judge, paid his fine for his fun like a little man and went on his way rejoicing. He may congratulate himself that his lines, while he was drunk, were cast in such a pleasant place as Wichita as there are but a few other places where that $500 bank roll would have been seen again. But the integrity of our police force has never been questioned."

Earp was embarrassed in early 1876, when his loaded single-action revolver fell out of his holster while he was leaning back on a chair and discharged when the hammer hit the floor. The bullet went through his coat and out through the ceiling.

Wyatt's stint as Wichita deputy came to a sudden end on April 2, 1876, when Earp took too active an interest in the city marshal's election. According to news accounts, former marshal Bill Smith accused Wyatt of using his office to help hire his brothers as lawmen. Wyatt got into a fistfight with Smith and beat him. Meagher was forced to fire and arrest Earp for disturbing the peace, which ended a tour of duty that the papers called otherwise "unexceptionable." When Meagher won the election, the city council was split evenly on re-hiring Earp. When his brother James opened a brothel in Dodge City, Kansas, Wyatt joined him.

After 1875, Dodge City, Kansas was at the end of the railroad line and became a major terminal for cattle brought up from Texas along the Chisholm Trail. Wyatt Earp was appointed assistant marshal in Dodge City under Marshal Larry Deger in 1876.

Earp spent the winter of 1876–77 in another boomtown, Deadwood City, Dakota Territory. He was not on the police force in Dodge City in late 1877, and rejoined the force in the spring of 1878. The Dodge newspaper reported in July 1878 that he had been fined $1.00 for slapping a muscular prostitute named Frankie Bell, who, according to the papers;

> "*She heaped epithets upon the unoffending head of Mr. Earp to such an extent as to provide a slap from the ex-officer.*"

Bell spent the night in jail and was fined $20.00, while Earp's fine was the legal minimum of $5.

In October 1877, Wyatt Earp left Dodge City to gamble throughout Texas. He stopped at Fort Griffin, Texas before returning to Dodge City in 1878 to become the assistant city marshal, serving under Charlie Bassett. He met John Henry "Doc" Holliday while he was there in Fort Griffin. In the summer of 1878, Holliday assisted Earp during a bar room confrontation when Wyatt *"was surrounded by desperadoes."* Earp credited Holliday with saving his life that day. They became friends as a result.

While in Dodge City, Wyatt became acquainted with Bat Masterson, his brother Jim Masterson, Luke Short and a sporting girl named Celia Anne "Mattie" Blaylock. She became Earp's companion until 1881. When Earp resigned from the Dodge City police force on September 9, 1879, she accompanied him to Las Vegas, New Mexico, and then Tombstone, Arizona.

At about 3:00 in the morning of July 26, 1878, while working as a lawman in Dodge City, George

Hoyt and other drunken cowboys shot their guns wildly, including three shots into the Comique Theater, causing comedian Eddie Foy to throw himself to the stage floor in the middle of his act. Fortunately, no one was injured. Assistant Marshal Earp and Policeman James Masterson responded and;

> *"Together with several citizens, they turned their pistols loose in the direction of the flying horsemen."*

As the riders crossed the bridge over the Arkansas River just a little south of town, George Hoyt fell from his horse from weakness caused by a wound in the arm he had received during the shooting fracas. Hoyt developed gangrene and died on August 21. Wyatt Earp claimed to have sighted Hoyt against the morning horizon and to have fired the fatal shot, but Hoyt could easily have been shot by Masterson or one of the citizens in the crowd.

Chapter Six

Wyatt's older brother Virgil was living in Prescott, Arizona Territory in 1879 and wrote Wyatt about the opportunities in the nearby silver-mining boom town of Tombstone. In the fall of 1879, Wyatt, his common-law wife Mattie Blaylock, his brother James and his wife, and Doc Holliday and his common-law wife Big Nosed Kate, all left for Arizona. They stopped in Las Vegas, New Mexico and at other locations, arriving in Prescott in November. The three Earp's moved with their wives to Tombstone, while Doc and Kate remained in Prescott where the gambling afforded better opportunities. Tombstone had grown from less than 100 people in March 1879 to about 1000 in less than a year. On November 27, 1879, three days before moving to Tombstone, Virgil Earp was appointed by Crawley P. Dakke, U.S. Marshal for the Arizona Territory, as Deputy U.S. Marshal for the Tombstone mining district, some 280 miles from Prescott. Deputy U.S. Marshal Dakke, whose office was in Tombstone, represented federal authority in the southeast area of the territory.

Wyatt brought horses and a buckboard wagon that he planned to convert into a stagecoach, but on arrival he found two established stage lines already running. In Tombstone, the Earp's staked mining claims and water rights interests, attempting to capitalize on the mining boom. Jim worked as a barkeep. On December 6, 1879, the three Earp's and Robert J. Winders filed a location notice for the First North Extension of the Mountain Maid Mine. When none of their business interests proved fruitful, Wyatt was hired in April or May 1880 by Wells Fargo & Company agent John Clum as a shotgun messenger on stagecoaches when they transported Wells Fargo strongboxes. In the summer of 1880, younger brothers Morgan arrived from Montana and Warren Earp moved to Tombstone as well. In September, Wyatt's friend Doc Holliday arrived from Prescott.

On July 25, 1880, Deputy U.S. Marshal Virgil Earp accused Frank McLaury of stealing six Army mules from nearby U.S. Army Camp Rucker. McLaury was a known associate of the Cowboy gang of cattle and horse rustlers. Legitimate cowmen were referred to as cattle herders or ranchers. Stealing the mules was a federal offense because the animals were U.S. property. U.S. Army Captain Hurst asked for Wyatt's assistance, and they caught the McLaurys in the act of changing the "U.S." brand to "D.8."

To avoid a gunfight, the posse withdrew with the understanding that the mules would be returned, but the mules were never returned to the Army. In response, Captain Hurst published an account of the loss of the mules in the papers, damaging Frank McLaury's reputation. Captain Hurst cautioned Wyatt, Virgil, and Morgan, that the cowboys had threatened their lives. A month later Wyatt Earp ran into Frank and Tom McLaury in Charleston, and they told him if he ever followed them again, as he had done before, they would kill him.

On July 28, Wyatt was appointed deputy sheriff for the eastern part of Pima County, which included Tombstone. Wyatt, however, only served for about three months. The deputy sheriff's position was worth more than US $40,000 a year (about $963,310 today) because he was also county assessor and tax collector, and the board of supervisors allowed him to keep ten percent of the amount paid.

On October 28, 1880, popular Tombstone town marshal Fred White attempted to break up a group of drunken revelers shooting at the moon late one night on Allen Street in Tombstone. Wyatt Earp was nearby, though unarmed. He borrowed a pistol from Fred Dodge and went to assist White. When White grabbed Curly Bill Brocius pistol, the gun discharged, striking White in the groin. Wyatt pistol-whipped Brocius, knocking him to the ground. Then he grabbed Brocius by the collar and told him to get up. Brocius protested in a drunken stupor;

"What have I done?"

Wyatt's coolness and nerve never showed to better advantage than they did that night. His voice was even, quiet as he spoke;

> *"When Morg and I reached him, Wyatt was squatted on his heels beside Curly Bill and Fred White. Curly Bill's friends were pot-shooting at him in the dark. The shooting was lively and slugs were hitting buildings and in all of noise that was being created by the shooting."*

Wyatt told his biographer, Stuart Lake, many years later that, he thought Brocious was still armed at the time and didn't see Brocius' pistol on the ground in the dark until afterward. The pistol contained one expended cartridge and five live rounds. Brocius waived a preliminary hearing so he and his case could be transferred to Tucson District Court. Virgil and Wyatt escorted Brocius to Tucson to stand trial, possibly saving him from a lynching. White, age 31, who died of his wound two days after his shooting.

On December 27, 1880, Wyatt testified that White's shooting was accidental. Curley Bill Brocius expressed regret, saying he had not intended to shoot White. It was also shown that Brocius' single action revolver could be fired when half-cocked. A statement from White before he died was introduced stating that the shooting was accidental. The judge ruled that the shooting was accidental and released Brocius. Brocius remained intensely angry about how Wyatt pistol whipped him and became an enemy to the Earps.

In the personal arena, 32-year-old Wyatt Earp and 35-year-old Johnny Behan shared an interest in the same beautiful 18-year-old woman, Josephine Sarah Marcus. She first visited Tombstone as part of the Pauline Markham Theatre Troupe on December 1, 1879 for a one-week engagement, the same day as Wyatt and his brothers arrived in town. Behan arrived in Tombstone in September 1880, and Marcus returned from a visit to San Francisco in October when they resumed their relationship.

In the summer of 1881, Josey Marcus found Behan in bed with the wife of a friend and kicked him out. Earp had until this time a common-law relationship with Mattie Blaylock, who was listed as his wife in the 1880 census. She suffered from severe headaches and became addicted to laudanum, a mixture of alcohol and opium, used as a pain killer in the Old West. The exact details of how Marcus and Wyatt developed a relationship are not known. Marcus and Wyatt went to great lengths to keep her name out of Lake's book, Wyatt Earp: Frontier Marshal and Marcus threatened litigation to keep it that way.

On the next page are two photos of Josephine Sarah Marcus, the first photo above at the age of

18, the second photo was taken at age 21. She came to Tombstone with a traveling acting troop. She was a dance girl and stage hand. She left a relationship with Cochise County Sheriff Johnny Behan for his political and personal antagonist Wyatt Earp.

The two pictures below of Josey Marcus were taken in Tombstone by the famous photographer C.S. Fly. There is no doubt that Josey was a beautiful woman

In the professional and political arena, Wyatt Earp, a Republican and Johnny Behan, a Democrat, competed for the position of Cochise County sheriff. The job was potentially very lucrative because the office holder was also county assessor and tax collector. The board of supervisors allowed the office holder to keep ten percent of the amounts paid.

Wyatt was initially appointed deputy sheriff by Cochise County Sheriff Charlie Shibell on July 28, 1880. Wyatt passed on his Wells Fargo job as shotgun messenger to Morgan. Wyatt did his job well, and from August through November his name was mentioned nearly every week by the Tombstone Epitaph or the Nugget newspapers.

In November, just three months later, Shibell ran for re-election against Republican challenger Bob Paul. Wyatt, favored Paul, and when Shibell won the election, Wyatt resigned on November 9, 1880, only twelve days after the White shooting. Shibell immediately appointed Behan as the new Pima deputy sheriff for eastern Pima County.

However, Bob Paul filed charges alleging that Cowboy supporters Ike Clanton, Curly Bill Brocius, and Frank McLaury had cooperated in ballot stuffing. Paul was eventually declared the winner of the Pima County sheriff election in April 1881. But by that time Paul could not replace Behan with Earp because on January 1, 1881, Cochise County was created out of the eastern portion of Pima County.

Both Earp and Behan applied to fill the new position of Cochise County sheriff. Earp thought he had a good chance to win the position because he was the former under sheriff in the region and a Republican, like Arizona Territorial Governor John C. Fremont. However, Behan had political influence in Prescott, where he served a term as Yavapai County Sheriff before moving to Tombstone.

Earp testified during the Spicer hearing after the Gunfight at the O.K. Corral that he and Behan had made a deal. If Earp withdrew his application to the legislature, Behan agreed to appoint Earp as his under sheriff. Behan received the appointment in February 1881, but did not keep his end of the bargain and instead chose Harry Woods. Behan testified that he had not made any deal with Earp, although later he admitted that he had lied. Behan said he broke his promise to appoint Earp because of an incident that occurred shortly before his appointment as Cochise County Sheriff.

This incident Behan spoke about arose after Earp learned that one of his prize horses, stolen more than a year before, was in the possession of Ike Clanton and his brother Billy. Earp and Holliday rode to the Clanton ranch near Charleston to recover the horse. On the way, they overtook Behan, who was riding in a buckboard. Behan was also heading to the ranch to serve an election-hearing subpoena on Ike Clanton. Accounts differ as to what happened next.

Wyatt Earp later testified that when he arrived at the Clanton ranch, Billy Clanton gave up the horse even before being presented with ownership papers. According to Behan's testimony, however, Earp had told the Clanton's that Behan was on his way to arrest them for horse theft. After the incident, which embarrassed both the Clanton's and Behan, Behan testified that he did not want to work with Earp and chose Woods instead.

Losing the under sheriff position, *(the man to become the next sheriff)*, left Wyatt Earp without a job in Tombstone; however, Wyatt and his brothers were beginning to make some money on their mining claims in the Tombstone area. In January 1881, Oriental Saloon owner Lou Rickabaugh gave Wyatt Earp a one-quarter interest in the faro concession at the Oriental Saloon in exchange for his services as a manager and enforcer. Wyatt invited his friend, lawman and gambler Bat Masterson, to Tombstone to help him run the faro tables in the Oriental Saloon. In June 1881, Wyatt also telegraphed another close friend, who was a deputy and lawman from Dodge City, Luke Short, who was living in Leadville, Colorado, and offered him a job as a faro dealer.

Bat Masterson remained in Tombstone until April, 1881, when he returned to Dodge City to assist his brother James, who had become the new town Marshal. On October 8, 1881 Doc Holliday got into a dispute with a local gambler, John Tyler in the Oriental Saloon. A rival gambling concession operator hired Tyler to make trouble at the Oriental and disrupt Wyatt's business. When Tyler started a fight after losing a bet, Wyatt threw him out of the saloon. Holliday later wounded Oriental owners Milt Joyce and his partner Lou Rickabaugh and was convicted of assault. Around this time Earp saved gambler Mike O'Rourke (aka; Johnny, Behind the Deuce, O'Rourke) from being hanged after he was arrested for murdering a miner. O'Rourke said he killed the miner in self-defense. Earp stood down a large crowd that wanted to lynch O'Rourke, an incident that added to Earp's legend as a lawman.

Tensions between the Earp's and both the Clanton's and McLaury's increased through 1881. On March 15, 1881 at 10:00 pm, three cowboys attempted to rob a Kinnear & Company stagecoach carrying $26,000 in silver bullion (about $626,152 in today's dollars) near Benson, Arizona, during which the popular driver Eli *"Bud"* Philpot and passenger Peter Roerig were killed.

The Earp's and a posse tracked the men down and arrested Luther King, who confessed he had been holding the reins for Bill Leonard, Harry "The Kid" Head, and Jim Crane as the robbers. King was arrested and Sheriff Johnny Behan escorted him to jail, but somehow King walked in the front door and almost immediately out the back door.

During the hearing into the Gunfight at the O.K. Corral, Wyatt testified that he offered the $3,600 in Wells Fargo reward money ($1,200 per robber) to

Ike Clanton and Frank McLaury in return for information about the identities of the three robbers. Wyatt testified that he had other motives for his plan as well: he hoped that arresting the murderers would boost his chances for election as Cochise County sheriff.

According to Wyatt Earp, both Frank McLaury and Ike Clanton agreed to provide information to assist in their capture, but never had a chance to fulfill the agreement. All three cowboy suspects in the stage robbery were killed when attempting other robberies. Wyatt told the court at the hearing after the O.K. Corral shootout that he had taken the extra step of obtaining a second copy of a telegram for Ike from Wells Fargo assuring that the reward for capturing the killers applied either dead or alive.

In his testimony at the court hearing, Clanton offered different testimony about the incident and accused Earp of leaking their deal to his brother Morgan or to Holliday. He said that Morgan Earp had asked him about whether he would make the agreement with Wyatt, and four or five days afterward Morgan confided in him that he and Wyatt had;

> *"Payed off $1,400 to Doc Holliday and Bill Leonard,"*

Who were supposed to be on the stage the night Bud Philpot was killed. During his testimony, Clanton told the court;

> *"I was not going to have anything to do with helping to capture the killers and then he corrected himself, kill Bill Leonard, Crane and Harr."*

49

Ike Clanton denied having any knowledge of the telegram confirming the reward money.

Meanwhile, tensions between the Earp's and the McLaury's increased with the holdup of another stage in the Tombstone area on September 8, this one a passenger stage in the Sandy Bob line, bound for nearby Bisbee. The masked robbers shook down the passengers and robbed the strongbox. They were recognized by their voices and language. They were identified as Pete Spence (an alias for Elliot Larkin Ferguson) and Frank Stilwell, a business partner of Spence who had shortly before been fired as a deputy of Sheriff Behan's (for county tax "accounting irregularities"). Spence and Stilwell were friends of the McLaury brothers. Wyatt and Virgil Earp rode with the sheriff's posse attempting to track the Bisbee stage robbers, and Wyatt discovered an unusual boot heel print in the mud. They checked with a shoemaker in Bisbee and found a matching heel that he had just removed from Stilwell's boot. A further check of a Bisbee corral turned up both Spence and Stilwell. Stilwell and Spence were arrested by sheriff's deputies Breckenridge and Nagel for the stage robbery, and later by Deputy U.S. Marshal Virgil Earp on the federal offense of mail robbery.

Released on bail, Spence and Stilwell were re-arrested by Virgil for the Bisbee robbery a month later, October 13, on the new federal charge of interfering with a mail carrier. The newspapers, however, reported that they had been arrested for a different stage robbery that occurred (October 8) near Contention City. Occurring less than two weeks before the O.K. Corral shootout, this final incident may have been misunderstood by the

McLaury's. While Wyatt and Virgil were still out of town for the Spence and Stilwell hearing, Frank McLaury confronted Morgan Earp, telling him that the McLaury's would kill the Earp's if they tried to arrest Spence, Stilwell, or the McLaury's again.

On Wednesday, October 26, 1881, the tension between the Earp's and the Cowboys came to a head. Ike Clanton, Billy Claiborne, and other Cowboys had been threatening to kill the Earp's for several weeks. Tombstone city Marshal Virgil Earp learned that the Cowboys were armed and had gathered near the O.K. Corral. He asked Wyatt and Morgan Earp and Doc Holliday to assist him, as he intended to disarm them. Wyatt was acting as a temporary assistant marshal, Morgan was a Deputy City Marshall, and Virgil deputized Holliday for the occasion. At approximately 3:00 p.m. the Earp's headed towards Fremont Street where the Cowboys had been reported gathering.

They confronted five Cowboys in a vacant lot adjacent to the O.K. Corral's rear entrance on Fremont street. The lot between the Harwood House and Fly's Boarding House and Photography Studio was narrow—the two parties were initially only about 6 to 10 feet (1.8 to 3.0 m) apart. Ike Clanton and Billy Claiborne fled the gunfight. Tom and Frank McLaury along with Billy Clanton were killed. Morgan was clipped by a shot across his back that nicked both shoulder blades and a vertebra. Virgil was shot through the calf and Holliday was grazed by a bullet.

On October 30, Ike Clanton filed murder charges against the Earp's and Holliday. Justice Spicer convened a preliminary hearing on October 31 to determine if there was enough evidence to go to trial. In an unusual proceeding, he took written and

51

oral testimony from a number of witnesses over more than a month.

Sheriff Behan, testifying for the prosecution, said;

> *"The Cowboys had not resisted arrest nor did they either throw up their hands. They turned out their coats to show they were not armed. He went on to say, Tom McLaury threw open his coat to show that he was not armed and that the first two shots were fired by the Earp party. Sheriff Behan insisted Doc Holliday had fired first using a nickel-plated revolver when he had been seen carrying a messenger shotgun immediately beforehand."*

The Earp's hired an experienced trial lawyer, Thomas Fitch, as defense counsel. Wyatt testified;

> *"I drew my gun only after Billy Clanton and Frank McLaury went for their pistols. He detailed the Earp's previous troubles with the Clanton's and McLaury's and explained that they intended to disarm the cowboys. He said they fired in self-defense."*

Fitch managed to produce testimony from prosecution witnesses during cross-examination that was contradictory and appeared to dodge his questions.

After extensive testimony, Justice Spicer ruled on November 30 that that there was not enough evidence to indict the men. He said the evidence indicated that the Earp's and Holliday acted within the law and that Holliday and Wyatt had been deputized temporarily by Virgil. Even though the

Earp's and Holliday were free, their reputations had been tarnished. Supporters of the Cowboys in Tombstone looked upon the Earp's as robbers and murderers and plotted revenge.

On December 28, while walking between saloons on Allen Street in Tombstone, Virgil was ambushed and maimed by a shotgun round that struck his left arm and shoulder. Ike Clanton's hat was found in the back of the building across Allen Street from where the shots were fired. Wyatt wired U.S. Marshal Crawley Dakke asking to be appointed deputy U.S. marshal with authority to select his own deputies. Dakke granted the request in late January and provided the Earp's with some funds he borrowed from Wells, Fargo & Company on behalf of the Earp's, variously reported as $500 to $3,000.

In mid-January, when Ally Rickabaugh sold the Oriental Saloon to Milt Joyce, Wyatt sold his gambling concessions at the hotel. The Earp's also raised some funds from sympathetic business owners in town. On February 2, 1882, Wyatt and Virgil, tired of the criticism leveled against them, submitted their resignations to Dakke, who refused to accept them because their accounts had not been settled.

On that same day, Wyatt sent a message to Ike Clanton that he wanted to reconcile their differences, which Clanton refused. Clanton was also acquitted that day of the charges against him in the shooting of Virgil Earp, when the defense brought in seven witnesses who testified that Clanton was in Charleston at the time of the shooting.

The Earp's needed more funds to pay for the extra deputies and associated expenses.

Contributions received from supportive business owners were not enough. On February 13, Wyatt mortgaged his home to lawyer James G. Howard for $365.00 (about $8,790 today) and received $365.00 in U.S. gold coins.

After attending a theatre show on March 18, Morgan Earp was assassinated by gunmen firing from a dark alley through a door window into room where he was playing billiards. Morgan was struck in the right side. The bullet shattered his spine, passed through his left side, and lodged in the thigh of George A. B. Berry. Another round narrowly missed Wyatt. A doctor was summoned and Morgan was moved from the floor to a nearby couch. The assassins escaped in the dark and Morgan died forty minutes later.

Wyatt Earp felt he could not rely on civil justice and decided to take matters into his own hands. He concluded that only way to deal with Morgan's murderers was to kill all who were involved in the death of his brother.

The day after Morgan's murder, Deputy U.S. Marshal Wyatt, his brother James, Doc Holliday, and a few others that Wyatt deputized took Morgan's body to the railhead in Benson. They put Morgan's body on the train with James, who accompanied it to the family home in Colton, California, where Morgan's wife waited to bury him. They guarded Virgil and Addie through to Tucson, where they had heard Frank Stilwell and other Cowboys were waiting to kill Virgil. The next morning Frank Stilwell's body was found alongside the tracks riddled with buckshot and gunshot wounds. Wyatt and five others were accused of murdering him and Tucson Justice of the Peace Charles Meyer issued warrants for their arrest.

The Earp posse briefly returned to Tombstone where Sheriff Behan tried to stop them. The heavily armed posse brushed him aside and set out for Pete Spence's wood camp in the Dragoon Mountains. They found and killed Florentino *"Indian Charlie"* Cruz. Two days later, near Iron Springs (later Mescal Springs), in the Whetstone Mountains, they were seeking to rendezvous with a messenger for them. They unexpectedly stumbled onto the wood camp of Curly Bill Brocius, Pony Diehl, Johnny Barnes and two other Cowboys. According to reports from both sides, the two sides immediately exchanged gun fire. Except for Wyatt and Texas Jack Vermillion, whose horse was shot, the Earp party withdrew to find protection from the heavy gunfire. Curly Bill fired at Wyatt with a shotgun but missed. Eighteen months prior Wyatt had protected Curly Bill against a mob ready to lynch him and then provided testimony that helped spare Curly Bill from a murder trial for killing Sheriff Fred White. Now, Wyatt returned Curly Bill's gunfire with his own shotgun and shot Curly Bill in the chest from about 50 feet away. Curly Bill fell into the water by the edge of the spring and died.

Wyatt received bullet holes in both sides of his long coat and another struck his boot heel. After emptying his shotgun, Wyatt fired his pistol, mortally wounding Johnny Barnes in the chest and wounded Milt Hicks in the arm. Vermillion tried to retrieve his rifle wedged in the scabbard under his fallen horse, exposing himself to the Cowboys' gunfire. Doc Holliday helped him gain cover. Wyatt had trouble remounting his horse because his cartridge belt had slipped down his legs. He was finally able to get on his horse and with the rest of the posse retreated.

The Earp Party rode north to the Percy Ranch, but was not welcomed by Hugh and Jim Percy, who feared the Cowboys; after a meal and some rest, they left at about 3:00 a.m. in the morning of March 27. The Earp party slipped into the area near Tombstone and met with supporters, including "Charlie" Smith and Warren Earp. On March 27, the posse arrived at the Sierra Bonita ranch of Colonel Henry C. Hooker, a wealthy and prominent rancher. That night Dan Tipton caught the first stage out of Tombstone and headed for Benson, carrying $1,000 from mining owner and Earp supporter E.B. Gage for the posse. Hooker congratulated Earp on the murder of Curly Bill. Hooker fed them and Wyatt told him he wanted to buy new mounts, but Hooker refused to take the money. When Behan's posse was observed in the distance, Hooker suggested Wyatt make his stand there, but Wyatt moved into the hills about three miles to nearby Reilly Hill.

The Earp posse did not meet with the posse, led by Cochise County Sheriff John Behan, searching for the Earp's, and in the middle of April 1882 the Earp party fled the Arizona territory, heading east into New Mexico Territory and then into Colorado.

The coroner reports credited the Earp party with killing four men in their two-week long ride. In 1888 Wyatt Earp gave an interview to California historian H. H. Bancroft during which he claimed to have killed *"over a dozen stage robbers, murderers, and cattle thieves"* in his time as a lawman.

The gunfight in Tombstone lasted only 30 seconds, but it would end up defining Earp for the rest of his life. After Wyatt killed Frank Stilwell in Tucson, his movements received national press coverage and he became a part of Western folklore.

Chapter Seven

After killing Curly Bill, the Earp's left Arizona for Colorado. They stopped in Albuquerque, New Mexico, where they met Deputy U.S. Marshal Bat Masterson, Wyatt's close old friend. The Earp's, Sherman McMasters, and Holliday rode with Masterson to Trinidad, Colorado where Masterson owned a saloon. Wyatt dealt Faro for several weeks before he, Warren, Holliday, and several others rode on to Gunnison, Colorado.

Doc Holliday headed to Pueblo and then Denver, Colorado. The Earp's and Texas Jack Vermillion set up camp on the outskirts of Gunnison, Colorado, where they remained for a couple of months quietly at first, rarely going into town for supplies.

Eventually, Wyatt took over a faro game at a local saloon. After Morgan Earp's death, Wyatt's former common-law wife, Celia Anne "Mattie" Blaylock, waited for him in Colton but eventually accepted that Wyatt was not coming back. Wyatt left Mattie their house when he left Tombstone. She moved to Globe, Arizona and resumed life as a prostitute. Wyatt instead went to San Francisco and joined Josephine, Warren and Virgil in late 1882. Josie, or Sadie as he called her, was his common-law wife for the next forty-six years. Mattie struggled with her addictions and committed "suicide by opium poisoning" on July 3, 1888. She is buried in the Globe Arizona City Cemetery.

On the next page is a copy of a photo found in our National Archives of the "Dodge City Peace Commission," Circa 1877. (L to R) standing: W.H. Harris, Luke Short, Bat Masterson, W.F. Petillon. Seated: Charlie Bassett, Wyatt Earp,

Frank McLain and Neal Brown.

On May 31, 1883, Earp returned along with Bat Masterson to Dodge City to help their friend Luke Short, who was a part owner of the Long Branch saloon, during what became known as the Dodge City War. When the Mayor tried to run Luke Short first out of business and then out of town, Short appealed to Masterson who contacted Earp. While Short was discussing the matter with Governor George Washington Glick in Kansas City, Kansas, his friends showed up in Dodge City to help Wyatt, Bat and Luke.

They were Johnny Millsap, Shotgun John Collins, Texas Jack Vermillion and Johnny Green. They marched up Front Street into Short's saloon where they were sworn in as deputies by constable *"Praire Dog"* Dave Marrow. The town council offered a compromise to allow Short to return for ten days to get his affairs in order, but Earp refused to compromise. When Short returned, there was no force ready to turn him away. Short's Saloon re-opened and the Dodge City War ended without a shot being fired.

Earp spent the next decade running saloons and gambling concessions and investing in mines in Colorado and Idaho, with stops in various boom towns. He also owned several saloons outright or in partnership with others.

In 1884, Wyatt and his wife Josie, Warren, James and Bessie Earp were in Eagle, Idaho, another mining boom town working at a saloon. Wyatt was looking for gold in the Murray-Eagle mining district. They opened a saloon called The White Elephant in a circus tent. An advertisement in a local newspaper suggests gentlemen 'come and see the elephant'.

Earp was named sheriff of the newly incorporated Kootenai County, Idaho. In Idaho Wyatt was involved in a brief shootout. On March 28, several feet of snow were still on the ground. Bill Buzzard, a miner of dubious reputation, began constructing a building when one of Wyatt's partners, Jack Enright, tried to stop the construction. Enright claimed the building was on part of his property. Words were exchanged and Buzzard reached for his Winchester. He fired several shots at Enright and a skirmish developed. Allies of both sides quickly took defensive positions between snow banks and began shooting at one another. Kootenai County Deputy Sheriff Wyatt Earp and Shoshone County Deputy W. E. Hunt ended the fight.

In about April 1885, it was reported that Wyatt Earp used his badge to join a band of claim jumpers in Embry Camp, later renamed Chewelah, Washington. Within six months their substantial stake had run dry, and the Earp's left the Murray-

Eagle district.

In 1885, Earp and Josie moved to San Diego, California where the railroad was about to arrive and a real estate boom was underway. They stayed for about four years. Earp speculated in San Diego's booming real estate market. Between 1887 and around 1896 he bought three saloons and gambling halls, one on Fourth Street and the other two near Sixth and E, all in the "respectable" part of town. They offered twenty-one games including faro, blackjack, poker, keno and other Victorian games of chance like pedro and monte. At the height of the boom, he made up to $1,000 a night in profit.

Wyatt particularly favored and may have run the Oyster Bar located in the Louis Bank of Commerce on Fifth Avenue. In 2003, the Oyster Bar saloon was converted into a restaurant by former San Diego mayor Roger Hedgecock who opened Roger's On Fifth. Wyatt had a long-standing interest in boxing and horse racing. In the 1887 San Diego City Directory he was listed as a capitalist or gambler. He won his first race horse "Otto Rex" and began investing in racehorses. He also judged prize fights on both sides of the border and raced horses. Earp was one of the judges at the County Fair races in Escondido in 1889.

The Earp's moved back to San Francisco in 1890 or 1893 so Josie could be closer to her family. Wyatt took a job managing a horse stable in Santa Rosa, California. Earp developed a reputation as a sportsman as well as a gambler. He won his first race horse, Otto Rex, in a card game. He owned a six-horse stable in San Francisco. At Santa Rosa, Earp personally competed in and won a harness race. From 1890 to 1897, they lived at four different residences in the city: 145 Ellis St., 720 McAllister St., 514A Seventh Ave. and 1004 Golden Gate Ave. Josephine wrote in I Married Wyatt Earp:

> "The Recollections of Josephine Sarah Marcus, that she and Wyatt were married in 1892 by the captain of multimillionaire Lucky Baldwin's yacht aboard his yacht. Raymond Nez wrote that his grandparents witnessed their marriage aboard a yacht off the California coast. Baldwin also owned the Santa Anita racetrack, which Wyatt, a long-time horse aficionado, frequented when they were in Los Angeles."

In the fall of 1897, Earp and Josie joined in the Alaska Gold Rush and headed for Nome, Alaska. He operated a canteen during the summer of 1899 and in September, Earp and partner Charles E. Hoxie built the Dexter Saloon in Nome, Alaska, the city's first two story wooden building and its largest and most luxurious saloon. The building was used for a variety of purposes because it was so large: 70 by 30 ff wide with 12 feet high ceilings. While there, Earp rubbed elbows with Jack London, future author Rex Beach, playwright Wilson Mizner, and Jack Dempsey's future boxing fight promoter Tex Rickard and Arizona Charlie Meadows. Wyatt was arrested twice in Nome for minor offenses.

On the next page is a photo of Wyatt Earp in taken in Nome, Alaska, found in our National Archives, with long-time friend former Tombstone mayor and editor of the Tombstone Epitaph newspaper, John Clum, Circa 1900

Wyatt and Josie returned to California in 1901 with an estimated $80,000. In February, 1902, they arrived in Tonopah, Nevada, where gold had been discovered and a boom was under way. He opened the Northern Saloon in Tonopah, Nevada and served as a deputy U.S. Marshal under Marshal J.F. Emmitt. His saloon, gambling and mining interests were profitable for a period.

A picture of Wyatt and Josie Earp in front of their Tonopah Saloon was found in our National Archives

After Tonapah, Nevada's gold strike boom waned, Wyatt staked mining claims just outside Death Valley and elsewhere in the Mohave Desert. In 1906 he discovered several deposits of gold and copper near the Sonoran Desert town of Vidal, California on the Colorado River and filed more than 100 mining claims near the Whipple Mountains. Wyatt and Josie Earp summered in Los Angeles and lived in at least nine small Los Angeles rentals as early as 1885 and as late as 1929, mostly in the summer. They bought a small cottage in Vidal and lived there during the fall, winter and spring months of 1925–1928, while he worked his *"Happy Days"* mines in the Whipple Mountains a few miles north. It was the only permanent residence they owned the entire time they were married. Wyatt had some modest success with the Happy Day Gold Mine and they lived on the slim proceeds of income from that and Kern County Oil.

In about 1910, when he was 62, the Los Angeles police department hired Wyatt and former Los Angeles detective Arthur Moore King at $10.00 per day to carry out various tasks "outside the law" such as retrieving criminals from Mexico, which he did very capably. This led to Wyatt's final armed confrontation. In October, 1910 he was asked by former Los Angeles Police Commissioner H. L. Lewis to head up a posse to protect surveyors of the American Trona Company who were attempting to wrest control of mining claims for vast deposits of potash on the edge of Searles Lake held in receivership by the foreclosed California Trona Company. Wyatt and the group he guarded were regarded as claim jumpers and were confronted by armed representatives of the other company. King wrote;

"The nerviest thing I ever saw was when Earp heard the commotion outside his tent with the claim jumpers threatening the mine employees with their guns pulled. Wyatt Earp came out of his tent with a Winchester rifle, firing a round at the feet of Federal Receiver Stafford W. Austin. He said back off or I'll blow you apart, or my name is not Wyatt Earp"

The owners summoned the U.S. Marshal who arrested Earp and 27 others, served them with a summons for contempt, and sent them home. Earp's actions did not resolve the dispute, which eventually escalated into the "Pot Ash Wars" of the Mojave Desert.

Wyatt and Josie Earp eventually moved to Hollywood, California and became a paid film consultant for several silent cowboy movies at the request of William S. Hart and Tom Mix. He met several well-known and soon to be famous actors on the sets of various movies. On the set of one movie, he met Marion Morrison (who later became famous under the assumed name of John Wayne). Morrison served Earp coffee on the sets, and later told Hugh O'Brien that he based his image of the Western lawman on his conversations with Earp. Director John Ford worked as an apprentice on the studio lots about the time that Wyatt Earp used to visit friends on the set, and Ford later claimed he reconstructed the Gunfight at the O.K. Corral based on Wyatt's input. In the early 1920s, Earp was given the honorary title of Deputy Sheriff in San Bernardino County, California.

The last surviving Earp brother and the last surviving participant of the Gunfight at the O.K.

Corral, Wyatt Earp died at home in the Earp's small apartment at 4004 W 17th Street, in Los Angeles, of chronic cystitis (some sources cite prostate cancer) on January 13, 1929 at the age of 80.

Wyatt Earp's pallbearers were prominent men: George W. Parsons, Charles Welch, Fred Dornberge, Los Angeles Examiner writer Jim Mitchell, Hollywood screenwriter Wilson Mizner, Earp's good friend from his days in Tombstone, John Clum, and Western actors William S. Hart and Tom Mix. Mitchell wrote Wyatt's obituary. The newspapers reported that Tom Mix cried during his friend's service. His wife Josie was too grief-stricken to attend. Josie had Earp's body cremated and buried Earp's ashes in the Marcus family plot at the Hills of Eternity in Colton, California.

Although it never was incorporated as a town, the settlement formerly known as Drennan located near the site of some of his mining claims was renamed Earp, California in his honor when the post office was established there in 1930.

When she died in 1944, Josie's ashes were buried next to Earp's. The original grave marker was stolen on July 8, 1957 but was later recovered. Their gravesite is the most visited resting place in the Jewish cemetery.

Wyatt is often viewed as the central character and hero of the Gunfight at the O.K. Corral, or at least in part because of all of his brothers, he was the only one who was never wounded nor killed. Wyatt Earp was never scratched, although his clothing was shot through with bullet holes. According to Flood's biography, Wyatt vividly recalled a presence that in several instances warned him away or urged him to take action. This happened when he was on the street, alone in his room at the Cosmopolitan Hotel, at Bob Hatch's Pool Hall, where he went moments before Morgan was murdered, and again when he approached Iron Springs and surprised Curly Bill Brocius started shooting at Earp and Holliday. Earp chased Brocius into Iron Springs and when Brocius turned and fired a shot at Earp, that missed, Wyatt Earp killed Curley Bill with a shotgun blast.

Like his brothers, Wyatt Earp was a physically imposing figure for his day: 6 feet tall, when most men were about 5 feet 6 inches. He weighed about 165 to 170 pounds, was broad-shouldered, long-armed, and all muscle. He was very capable of using his fists instead of his weapon to control those resisting his authority, and was reputed to be an expert with a pistol. He showed no fear of any man. The Tombstone Epitaph said of Wyatt;

> *"Bravery and determination were requisites, and in every instance proved him the right man in the right place."*

Virgil Earp actually held the legal authority in Tombstone the day of the shoot out. Virgil was both Tombstone City Marshall and Deputy U.S. Marshal. Virgil had considerably more experience with weapons and combat as a Union soldier in the Civil War, and in law enforcement as a sheriff, constable, and marshal than did Wyatt. As city marshal, Virgil made the decision to disarm the Cowboys in Tombstone. Wyatt was only a temporary assistant marshal to his brother. But because Wyatt outlived Virgil and due to a creative biography written by Stuart Lake that made Wyatt famous, his name became well-known and the subject of many movies, television shows, biographies and works of fiction.

Public perception of Wyatt Earp's life has varied over the years as media accounts of his life have changed. The stories of the Earp brother's actions in Tombstone were published by newspapers nationwide mostly due to the reporters from the Tombstone Epitaph newspaper that covered their every move. When citizens of Dodge City learned the Earp's had been charged with murder after the gunfight, they sent letters endorsing and supporting the Earp's to Judge Wells Spicer.

Among his peers, Wyatt was respected. His deputy Jimmy Cairns described Wyatt's work as a police officer in Wichita, Kansas;

> *"Wyatt Earp was a wonderful officer. He was game to the last ditch and apparently afraid of nothing. The cowmen all respected him and seemed to recognize his superiority and authority at such times as he had to use it. He was the most dependable man I ever knew; a quiet, unassuming chap who never drank and in all respects a clean young fellow."*

John Clum, the owner of The Tombstone Epitaph newspaper at the time the Earp's were in Tombstone, and mayor of Tombstone while Wyatt was a gambler and lawman there, described him in his book It All Happened in Tombstone.

> *"Wyatt's manner, though friendly, suggested a quiet reserve… Frequently it has happened that men who have served as peace officers on the frontier have craved notoriety in connection with their dealings with the outlaw element of their time. Wyatt Earp deprecated such*

notoriety, and during his last illness he told me that for many years he had hoped the public would weary of the narratives, distorted with fantastic and fictitious embellishments, that were published from time to time concerning him, and that his last years might be passed in undisturbed obscurity."

Author Bill Dixon, who knew Wyatt early in his adult life wrote;

"Wyatt Earp was a shy young man with few intimate friends. With casual acquaintances he seldom spoke unless spoken to. When he did say anything it was to the point, without fear or favor, which wasn't relished by some; but that never bothered Wyatt. To those who knew him well he was a genial companion. He had the most even disposition I ever saw; I never knew him to lose his temper. He was more intelligent, better educated, and far better mannered than the majority of his associates, which probably did not help them to understand him. His reserve limited his friendships, but more than one stranger, down on his luck, has had firsthand evidence of Wyatt's generosity. I think his outstanding quality was the nicety with which he gauged the time and effort for every move. That, plus his absolute confidence in him, gave him the edge over the run of men."

Famous lawman Bat Masterson a lifelong friend of Wyatt Earp described Wyatt Earp in 1907;

"Wyatt Earp was one of the few men I personally knew in the West in the early days whom I regarded as absolutely destitute of physical fear. I have often remarked, and I am not alone in my conclusions, that what goes for courage in a man is generally fear of what others will think of him - in other words, personal bravery is largely made up of self-respect, egotism, and apprehension of the opinions of others. Wyatt Earp's daring and apparent recklessness in time of danger is wholly characteristic; personal fear doesn't enter into the equation, and when everything is said and done, I believe he values his own opinion of himself more than that of others, and it is his own good report he seeks to preserve... He never at any time in his career resorted to the pistol excepting cases where such a course was absolutely necessary. Wyatt could scrap with his fists, and had often taken all the fight out of bad men, as they were called, with no other weapons than those provided by nature."

After the shootout in Tombstone, his pursuit and murder of those who attacked his brothers, and after leaving Arizona, Wyatt was often in doubt about the public's perception of his and his brothers' reputation. His role in history has stimulated considerable ongoing scholarly and editorial debate. A large body of literature has been written about Wyatt Earp and his legacy, some of it highly fictionalized. Considerable portions of it are either full of admiration and flattery or hostile debunking.

Wyatt was repeatedly criticized in the media over the remainder of his life. His wife Josephine wrote;

> *"The falsehoods that were printed in some of the newspapers about him and the unjust accusations against him hurt Wyatt more deeply than anything that ever happened to him during my life with the him, with the exception of his mother's death and that of his father and brother, Warren.*

On March 12, 1922, the Sunday Los Angeles Times ran a scandalous article by J.M. Scanland about Wyatt's life as a lawman. During the same year, Frederick R. Bechdolt published When the West Was Young, a story about Wyatt's time in Tombstone, but he mangled many basic facts. He described the Earp-Clanton differences as the falling out of partners in crime. Both of these reports bothered Wyatt a great deal, but he remained stalwart. In 1924, a story in a San Francisco paper said interviewing him was "like pulling teeth." Wyatt Earp didn't trust the press and he preferred to keep his mouth shut.

In late 1899, Wyatt opened a gambling concession in Seattle, Washington. On November 25, the local paper, the Seattle Star, described Wyatt Earp;

> *"A man of great reputation among the toughs and criminals, inasmuch as he formerly walked the streets of a rough frontier mining town with big pistols stuck in his belt, spurs on his boots and a devil-may-care expression upon his official face."*

Below is the last known photo of Wyatt Earp taken at home in Colton, CA on August 9, 1923, at age 75. This photo was found in our National Archives.

Wyatt Earp died on January 13, 1929 at the age of 80. His funeral pallbearers were his best friends. From left to right in the photo below are: W.J. Hunsaker, George Parsons, John Clum, Silent Film western Actor, William S. Hart, Wilson Mizner, and the famous Film Western Actor of all time Tom Mix. This photo is from our National Archives.

Chapter Eight

After finishing Wyatt Earp's short biography, we are now going to get back to the Heavyweight Championship fight between the lower ranked contender Tom Sharkey and the Champion Bob Fitzsimmons that occurred in San Francisco, California on Wednesday December 2, 1896.

Once the haggling was over picking the referee and the other issues that needed to be settled, the fight was on for that night. Both Tom Sharkey and Bob Fitzsimmons appeared to be in great physical condition. The stiff contest that followed revealed that both men were well matched, although in point of fairness and style it was obvious that Bob Fitzsimmons was in far better shape than Tom Sharkey.

It had been advertised, that many women would see this fight. There were a few sandwiched about, some in a sub gallery, shadowed by seats and closely escorted, a closely yelled pair in a lower box seat, and another feminine couple minus their hats, in another box seat. The male ushers were dressed in black pants and a matching sport coat. The female ushers were appropriately dressed in black evening dresses.

Before the fight ever took place though, it must be clear on how Wyatt Earp became the referee. The two corner men and their managers debated on who should referee the bout. No matter what referee name was suggested the other would dispute. Sharkey's manager, Lynch, offered the name of his famous friend, Wyatt Earp. Fitzsimmons manager, Martin Julian, questioned whether Earp had experience. Lynch stated that Earp had refereed in thirty professional bouts, taking place including Los Angeles, San Diego and Arizona. Julian hesitantly at first but then agreed that Wyatt Earp would be a perfect referee.

When Earp was approached for the job, he flat turned them down. After many conversations with Martin Julian, Earp finally decided to take the job. Four hours before the bout, several East Coast patrons and local San Franciscan's, approached Martin Julian to warn him that Wyatt Earp had been paid off and that he would not allow Fitzsimmons to win. The next 3-4 hours are chaotic. Martin Julian wanted Earp dismissed as the referee. Dan Lynch vehemently disagreed. The two sides disputed the pick of Earp as referee until the fight began.

Fitzsimmons entered the ring to polite applause. Sharkey entered the ring to a thunderous ovation, especially from $2 back seat crowd. The boxers shook hands. Referee Earp had been handed a certified $10,000 check to be given to the winner. In those days the referee was also the judge. Unlike today when the referee's job is only to referee the fight and the three judges determine the winner of the fight on a point system. With pugilists and the referee inside the ring, Martin Julian climbed through the ropes and entered the ring. Next came the sound of the bell at ten thirty that evening signally that the fight was about to begin. Below is the synopsis of each round reported by a Ring Magazine writer and then the view of the fight in italics after each round, that was reported by Nellie Davis;

Round 1: Sharkey bobs head and gloves – steps forward and throws right to head – misses – throws left to head – misses.   Sharkey backs –

73

bobs head and gloves – steps forward and lands left to body – backs. Sharkey bobs head and gloves – steps forward and throws left to head – misses. The Champion counters with high left jab to head – misses. Sharkey pauses – bobs head and gloves – charges forward to throw a left punch. Champion Fitz expects and throws short left jab that lands to face – follows with right that lands to jaw – Sharkey knocked to ground. Sharkey rises – a bit dazed as he covers up – backs. Champion steps forward – a couple left feints – Sharkey bobs head and attempts to cover. Champion throws left half hook that lands to jaw – Sharkey flops backward to ground – slightly tangled in lower ropes. Fitzsimmons assists Sharkey until the Irishman staggers back to his feet.

Nellie Verrill Mighels Davis a woman sportswriter for the nationally syndicated newspaper the Carson City Appeal reports;

> *"At the end of the first round there were two sleek, shining bodies, glazed with sweat and shining in the fierce light. Sharkey's chest was heaving like a draught horse and he seemed much the wearier of the two. Fitzsimmons was looking about the crowd while he stood tall on his feet in the corner waiting for the next round to begin."*

Round 2: The Champion is anxious to begin round. He paces and fidgets as he waits... Bell sounds... Champion steps out – feints left to head – follows with left that lands to forehead. Sharkey attempts to step forward and throw a right to head – misses wildly – Fitz steps back to easily evade.

Nellie Verrill Mighels Davis the sportswriter stated while waiting the bell for the third round to begin;

> "The button is pressed again and they begin to dance about to the quickstep: Fitz came over three quarters of the way, and after feinting tries the left at the head. Sharkey ducked and caught him around the legs."

Round 3: Sharkey bobs head and gloves – springs forward as he attempts to club top of head with left – misses – throws desperate right to top of head – misses as Champion evades. An aggressive Sharkey steps forward and lands a left to body. Champion counters with a right punch that landed to Sharkey's face. Sharkey throws right to head – misses while stumbling. Champion head bobs and steps away. Sharkey regains balance – bobs head and gloves – steps forward to throw left – Champion stops foe with left jab that lands to head. Sharkey bobs head and gloves – steps forward to throw left – Champion easily lands left jab to forehead instead. Sharkey bobs head and gloves – madly charges forward and lands left to body – tries to follow with right but loses balance. Champion attempts to evade and throw left jab – misses. Sharkey charges forward and lands illegal right to crotch – crowd boos.

Again waiting for the bell for the next to begin, Nellie Verrill Mighels Davis again wrote;

> *"The suspicious blows were, however due to Sharkey's style of swinging. Being so short, he hit in a circular way at Fitzsimmons and when that wily boxer ducked away from him blows that were aimed high at the body struck far*
> *below the mark."*

Round 4: Sharkey bobs head and gloves – charges forward and throws left to head – misses as the Champion evades – throws right to head – misses as the Champion evades – throws left to head – misses as the Champion evades. Sharkey steps forward aggressively and pushes the Champion backward onto his butt (no knockdown). Sharkey is tired and attempts to land a cheap shot left to head. Champion evades while on the ground. Sharkey throws an illegal right to head. Champion evades and rises to his feet. Champion grabs and holds the out of control Irishman. The crowd is yelling with mixed frenzy. Sharkey's supporters mistakenly believe the illegal push was a knockdown. Champion's supporters are angry at the fouls and attempt to illegally hit someone who is on the ground. Sharkey bobs head and gloves – steps forward – Champion Fitz awaits and lands an over the top left hook to head. Sharkey bobs head and gloves – charges forward and grabs the Champion in a clinch. Sharkey holds and bulls the Champion back to ropes – tries to illegally pin and punch – lands right to lower body – lands right to lower body. Champion lands a short left jab to head and escapes Sharkey's hold.

Waiting between rounds for the bell to start the fifth round, Nellie Verrill Mighels Davis the woman sportswriter wrote her synopsis of the round;

"In the fourth round, Sharkey pushed Fitz over on the floor and before Bob could get up, made a couple of vicious swipes at him. Fitz cleverly clinched and avoided damage, but it was a clear case of a foul on Sharkey's part."

Round 5: Sharkey's face is covered with blood. His left eye is partially closed. Fitzsimmons determinedly steps forward with bobbing head and gloves. Champion throws a right at the bobbing head – misses. Champion steps forward to throw a left – Sharkey rises from his crouch and lands hard left jab to head – his supporters roar. Champion feints a left to head. Champion throws and lands a left to face. A confused Sharkey attempts to back. Champion aggressively steps forward with a right that lands to jaw – Sharkey was knocked to the ground – tangled in lower ropes. (This is the 3rd knockdown of Sharkey with no published account that referee Earp has initiated any sort of '10' count). Champion protects Sharkey from slipping out of the ring as he assists the Irishman to his feet.

A different sportswriter who was at the fight submitted his resume of the fight round and is below;

"In the fifth round Sharkey fell through the ropes clumsily and Fitzsimmons helped him back. In the fifth, Sharkey did more mean work, grabbing Fitz around the legs and trying to throw him…. A poke on the nose and a left swing on the jaw sent Sharkey down. He rolled under the ropes and would have gone off the platform had not Bob courteously hauled him back. It was obvious at this point that Sharkey was losing steam was evident. He clinched at every opportunity, striking interlocked, contrary to agreement."

Again waiting between rounds for the bell to start the sixth round Nellie Verrill Mighels Davis, the sportswriter from the Carson City Appeal, wrote her synopsis of the fifth round;

"It seemed as if Sharkey could not help fouling. Not once but a dozen times he wrestled the Australian, butted him with his shoulders and grasped his legs as he tried to hurl him over his head.... Fitz let the sailor have his left and right in the jaw, knocking him through the ropes in a very bad condition. So close was Sharkey to the edge of the platform that he looked as if he might fall off. Fitzsimmons with the coolness of an old respectable professional classy fighter reached out and caught him and pulled him into the ring."

Round 6: Champion throws a right to foe's bobbing head – misses. Champion throws a left to head – misses the ducking Irishman. Champion lands a left to head. Sharkey charges forward and grabs the Champion around the legs. Champion is enraged at the persistent illegal tactics against him. Champion steps forward to punch. Sharkey backs. Champion continues forward. Sharkey surges forward and clinches.

Nellie Verrill Mighels Davis the sportswriter again reports in her notes on the sixth round;

"At each round and during it and all the time the crowd yelled madly, with hats and arms in air. It was like 10,000 maniacs, each man yelling for his favorite and his money. As the rounds reeled off, with Sharkey still in the ring, the men who bet on his endurance went crazy with joy."

Round 7: Sharkey bobs head and gloves – charges forward. Champion leads with a left jab feint – lands right to head – lands left uppercut to jaw – lands right uppercut to jaw. Sharkey continues to foolishly step forward. An enraged Sharkey surges ahead and grabs the Champion with a wrestling clinch. Both boxers grapple while attempting to punch. The bell sounds. Champion releases his clinch at the conclusion of the round. Champion turns his back on the Irishman as he returns to his corner. Sharkey illegally charges an opponent that is not looking and throws right to the back of head. Champion evades. Sharkey illegally throws a left to head – misses…. (There is no published account of referee Earp having issued a single warning to Sharkey for these repeated cheap shot fouls).

Again while waiting for the start of the seventh round Nellie Verrill Mighels Davis sportswriter again reports her synopsis of the seventh round;

"Fitz is after the marine like a tiger. Sharkey won't let go of a clinch. Fitz is

looking for a good opening to jab that left in. He finally finds it and lands both hands. Sharkey gets the better of the mix-up. He is fighting foul. Fitz is not as fast in this round and the sailor lands frequently."

"Fitz swung his right repeatedly for the jaw, but in some manner Sharkey escaped. The left jabs always connected, though, and Tom was decidedly on the wane. Bob himself was none too strong and seemed to be a bit tired when the round closed."

Round 8: Champion lands a straight left jab to head – Sharkey wobbles backward. Champion pursues and lands a right to the top of his crouching foe's head. Sharkey backs near the ropes. Champion throws a left hook to head – misses. Sharkey bobs head and evades. The Irishman is desperate as he clinches around the waist. Champion attempts to shake himself free. Sharkey will not let go of his hold. Referee Earp intervenes. Earp is unsuccessful as he fails to separate the boxers. Earp finally pushes the boxers apart. Sharkey staggers toward the center ring and halts. The outmatched Irishman attempts to be defensive and protect his face. Champion lands a left jab to stomach. Champion lands another left jab to stomach and backs. Sharkey wobbles forward though he is unable to defend himself. Sharkey attempts to keep his gloves upward. Champion steps forward and lands hard left to exposed stomach – Sharkey's gloves drop. Champion follows with a right uppercut that lands to chin – Sharkey collapses to the ground.

The crowd is in pandemonium. Referee Earp is not offering a count. Sharkey noisily writhes on the floor as if fouled. Twenty seconds have elapsed with no count or signal. The San Francisco crowd roars its approval at the apparent knockout. Sharkey stops moving. Champion Fitzsimmons raises his gloves in triumph. The Champion waves his glove in acknowledgment of the appreciative crowd. Sharkey's corner man, Lynch, enters the ring and shouts conversation with referee Earp. Several seconds pass. Lynch shakes his fist in triumph but no one notices. Another 30 seconds elapse before it is announced to the crowd that the Champion has been disqualified. Sharkey is declared the victor. Chaos ensues. Boos and hisses shower from all directions. Fitzsimmons entered the ring favored to win, but not the crowd favorite. Referee Earp frantically waves his hands toward the hostile, threatening crowd. Earp receives hate and invective, threats and curses, "FRAUD" and "FIX" and "CHEAT" are shouted at him. The famous gunfighter is frightened as he wisely exits. Sharkey still lay on the ground. This is usually the moment when a boxing mob attempts 'humanity' by quieting and showing concern for a fallen or injured pugilist. But with referee Earp gone, shouts and curses, boos and hisses, are aimed at Sharkey and his corner men.

Nellie Verrill Mighels Davis the sportswriter for the San Francisco Examiner again reports in her notes on the seventh and final round;

"It appeared to be a lame conclusion. Sharkey fell over like a collapsed balloon. He writhed in pain, where a moment before he had been fresh and strong. They carried him out – the man who had been like a lion, while Fitzsimmons friends shouted that he was shamming, and the sailors supporters swore he was not, until for a moment it looked like a hundred fights all over the house. Fitzsimmons paced about the ring shaking his fist, spitting his rage, and the crowd stood up in its chairs, everybody talking at the top of his voice, with the decision in doubt because no one would listen. The referee had vanished like the Arabian Genie."

Tom Sharkey post bout comment;

"I am certain that Fitzsimmons fouled me deliberately to save himself from defeat. It was getting too plain to him that I was gaining in strength, while he was going down hill, so to speak, so he thought he would lose on a foul."

Bob Fitzsimmons post bout comment;

"He fouled me at every clinch. I appealed eight times, and then, seeing that it was no use protesting, I quit and went in hitting my man just where I wanted to. In the fifth round Sharkey

83

clinched and caught me round the hips. The referee deliberately stuck his fingers in my face, cutting my eyelid with his nails."

W.H. Naughton (boxing writer);

"If Fitzsimmons struck Sharkey a foul blow last night I did not see it. But even at that I would scarcely like to go on record as saying that the punch on which the fight was given the sailor was not foul."

The San Francisco Chronicle;

"It was Bob Fitzsimmons hand that struck the $10,000 blow last night, but the referee – none other than Wyatt Earp, who is better known in gun fighting circles than to pugilism – called it a foul and gave the trophy of battle, a certified check for a little fortune, to the sailor fighter who lay hopelessly knocked out in his corner of the ring."

The Brooklyn Daily Eagle reported;

"Then Fitz got up to finish the job in a workmanlike manner. A right half arm jolt under the chin sent the sailor's head to one side. A left hook similarly applied sent him over backward. Then came the much disputed foul. Very few of the immense crowd could be convinced that Fitz had been unfair and it is almost certain that if a foul were committed, it was unintentional."

84

The San Francisco Chronicle;

> *"There was pandemonium of shouting from the short enders who hadn't looked for anything beyond winnings on the rounds and a fierce, long sustained deep-throated yell of a fraud job and robbery."*
>
> *This man Sharkey, who they claim was so badly knocked out, actually took the check out of the referee's hand and stuck it in his belt directly after he fell down."*
>
> *Amid the deafening roar of the crowd Danny Needham leaped into the ring shouting, "Foul!" His words were lost in the tumult. The referee finished the count. Then the referee bent over the prostrate man, lifted his hand, indicating Sharkey the winner on a low blow. As Sharkey's seconds lifted him through the ropes and hurried him to his dressing room, Wyatt Earp handed Sharkey's manager the $10,000 winners take check to him.*

By that time the crowd was quiet, waiting for a further announcement. Wyatt Earp climbed through the ropes, strode up the aisle and into his dressing room, leaving the astounded Fitzsimmons standing unhurt in the ring. The spectators were still waiting for a full explanation of the decision. Only after Earp had left the ring did the crowd realize what had happened. The curses and cries "fix" were mingled in the crowd as they finally realized the shocking knowledge that the referee had made the call and that he had the last word.

Referee Wyatt Earp's post fight statement from his dressing room follows;

"Julian came to me before the fight and said he had been told I was fixed. I am a friend of Lynch to be sure, but I know Sharkey only slightly. I first met him the night before he fought Corbett. Fitzsimmons I met four years ago, and I was introduced to him by Bat Masterson, the best friend I have on earth. If I had any leanings they would be toward Fitzsimmons, for I know that Bat Masterson, who is in Denver tonight, had every dollar he had bet on Fitzsimmons."

Below is a copy of the original signed check, published in the San Francisco Examiner, on December 5, 1896.

FAC-SIMILE OF THE CHECK THAT SHARKEY HOPES TO CASH.

Controversial $10,000 check as shown in San Francisco newspaper.

,

This one was a damn brawl, was a statement that was heard from someone in the audience. Some of the folks that were ringside swore they saw the foul very clearly. The reporters were busy comparing notes, trying to figure out if anyone had actually seen a foul blow struck. Fitzsimmons was stalking the ring while Julian screamed at the crowd and the ring officials.

Lynch would not allow anyone to enter Tom Sharkey or Wyatt Earp's dressing rooms after the fight, not even the doctor that was summoned to treat Sharkey.

The photo below of the fight was taken at ringside, and that appeared in the San Francisco Examiner. Referee Wyatt Earp is the man wearing the suspenders and bow tie. Bob Fitzsimmons is pictured on the right having just thrown an overhand right and Tom Sharkey is in the middle plodding into Fitz and throwing a counter straight right punch.

The Massillon Ohio Independent Newspaper, December 7, 1896, reported on the fight. Other than a few differences, it coincides with the report by Mighels Davis;

SHARKEY WON ON FOUL

Fitzsimmons Defeated at San Francisco

TALKS WITH THE PRINCIPALS

Sharkey Says He Would Have Knocked Fitzsimmons Out Had the Battle Continued.

The Latter Charges Conspiracy

Earp Explains the Foul By Associated Press to the Independent

San Francisco, December 5- 1896- Referee Earp gave the decision to Sharkey in the fight between the sailor and Fitzsimmons, claiming that while Sharkey was falling away from Fitzsimmons's left hand on the chin that Fitz struck Sharkey in the groin with his knee. They fought eight rounds.

Referee Wyatt Earp, who was openly charged with purposely giving Sharkey the fight as determined on beforehand, says the first time his honor has been questioned. He saw the foul below the belt. He says he should have given the fight in an earlier round, when Fitzsimmons landed a left handed blow and returned with his elbow cutting Sharkey's eye brow open.

Sharkey says: "Fitzsimmons deliberately fouled me to save himself from defeat. I would soon have conquered Fitz if not fouled. I am ready to meet him again."

The foul, if foul it was, could not be seen from the press stand, but Referee Earp gave his decision in spite of Fitz's protests.

It was Fitz's fight from the start to finish. He fought fairly, while the sailor continually used foul tactics. He would clinch and lift Fitz from his feet, strike in the clinch, though the men had previously agreed not to do so, and he was generally unfair.

Fully 15,000 people saw the fight. Forty thousand dollars was taken in at the box office for the fight. Several hundred ladies were present.

Wyatt Earp, the referee, was a famous Arizona stage driver, who has figured in many a gun fight on the border.

Julian, Fitzsimmons' backer, at first refused to accept Earp, owing to rumors of crookedness, but finally Fitzsimmons himself gave in.

THE FIGHT BY ROUNDS

Round 1- The men advance to the center of the ring and sparred for a moment. Fitzsimmons led several times with his left, but Sharkey was able to get away from the punches. Fitzsimmons landed lightly with a right on the head, Sharkey clinches. Sharkey swings his left at Fitz's body and a moment later landed a hard left punch on Fitz's neck.

Sharkey landed a right and left on Fitz's head, and ducked a vicious left swing from Fitz. Sharkey then threw a right toward Fitz's head but Fitz got

89

away. Sharkey then rushed Fitz and threw a left hand at Fitz's body that landed. Fitz knocks Sharkey down with a right to his jaw. The round ended with Sharkey in the corner and Fitz trying to hit him again in the head.

Round 2- Fitz standing before time is called. Men sparred and Fitz landed a light left on Sharkey's face. Sharkey rushed, but Fitz clinched. Fitz swings right and left but misses. Sharkey landed a hard left to Fitz's chest. Fitz tried a left to Sharkey's face, but got hit with a light left on his head. Fitz ducked a hard left from Sharkey. Sharkey ducked a hard left from Fitz and then clinched. Fitz swung a hard right but the punch missed its target and then he landed a left on Sharkey's head. Then Fitz landed a hard right to Sharkey's body. Sharkey missed a right and left to Fitz's head. Sharkey landed a right and left on the head and neck of Fitz, and then received two punches from Fitz. Fitz ducked a return right hand punch from Sharkey. Fitz tries a left to Sharkey's head and misses. Round tow ends with Fitz the aggressor.

Round 3-Fitz rushes across the ring toward Sharkey, but Sharkey ducks and clinches low. Sharkey tried to throw a left for Fitz's body that misses and he clinches. Fitz swings a right and a left that land on Sharkey's head. Sharkey returns by swinging both a left and right that land on Fitz's face but cause very little damage. Fitz staggered Sharkey with a straight right to Sharkey's head. Sharkey returns by swinging a left that lands on Fitz's face. Fitz again swings with a left and right but Sharkey ducks both punches. Sharkey doing most of the leading swinging wildly as Fitz looked like he was waiting to land another big right uppercut. The round ends with both men in a clinch.

Round 4- Sharkey plods to the middle of the ring and meets Fitz with a left hand that knocks Fitz down. Then Sharkey ducks a left from Fitz and counters with a right and left of his own, that lands on Fitz's body. Fitz starts fighting carefully. Sharkey ducks a right from Fitz but Fitz lands a left and Sharkey counters with a left to Fitz's head and puts Fitz on the ropes. Fitz clinches. Fitz tried a left and right to Sharkey's body but misses both punches. Sharkey tries a right and then lands a left to Fitz's head, staggering Fitz. Fitz swings a right and left defensive punch that land on Sharkey's head and stagger him. The round ends with both men against the ropes.

Round 5- Both men stand up before the call of time. Fitz tried a right to Sharkey's head as they met in the middle of the ring. Sharkey started bleeding from a cut over his left eye. Fitz lands a left hook to Sharkey's face. Fitz tries a left hook and misses. Fitz swings a hard right and left that land on Sharkey's face. Sharkey ducks after receiving the punches and clinches.

91

Sharkey then lands two hooks to Fitz's face. Fitz counters by landing a right to Sharkey's head. In the next scrimmage Fitz lands a hard right to Sharkey's face and knocks him to the canvass. As Sharkey gains gets to his feet, Fitz tries to hit him again but Sharkey grabs Fitz and clinches. This clinch was to avoid anymore of Fitz's big blows. Sharkey falls under the ropes from the punches and Fitz kindly assisted him back through the ropes and to his feet. The fifth round ends with both men in a clinch,

Round Six and Seven were in favor of Fitz, as Sharkey fouled Fitz considerably.

Round 8- Fitzsimmons leads with a left for Sharkey's face and misses as they meet in the middle of the ring, but an instant later Fitz lands a right on Sharkey's head Sharkey clinches and rushes Fitz pinning him on the ropes. Fitz tries a right and left while against the ropes. Sharkey lands a left to Fitz's head. Fitz swings with a right landing on Sharkey's head. Then he hits Sharkey with a left uppercut and follows with a right to Sharkey's head. After two minutes of challenger Tom Sharkey avoiding Fitzsimmons in the eighth round, Fitz catches up with Sharkey and lands a hard right to Sharkey's jaw that puts Sharkey to the floor with a smash. Fitz as Sharkey rises from the canvas jolts Sharkey under the chin with his left and the sailor went over backwards. As

Sharkey fell he put his hand to his groin.
He made no attempt to rise & carried
unconscious from ring.

Bob Fitzsimmons was favored to win, and bets flowed heavily his way. Wyatt entered the ring still armed with his Colt .45 and had to be disarmed. He later said he forgot he was wearing it. Fitzsimmons carried the fight until the eighth round when Wyatt stopped the bout on a foul, ruling that Fitzsimmons had hit Sharkey when he was down. His ruling was greeted with loud boos and catcalls. Wyatt Earp based his decision on the Marquis of Queensbury rules, which state in part;

> *"If a man on one knee, he is considered down and if struck is entitled to the stakes."*

Very few witnessed the foul Earp ruled on. He awarded the decision to Sharkey, who attendants carried out as;

> *"As limp as a rag."*

Fitzsimmons obtained an injunction against distributing the prize money until the courts could determine who the rightful winner was. The judge ruled that prize fighting was illegal in San Francisco and the courts would not determine who really won the fight. The decision provided no vindication for Earp and he soon left San Francisco for good. The San Francisco papers lampooned and scrutinized Wyatt for a full month, questioning his honesty. The San Francisco Call vilified him, calling him a crook and a cheat. Earp was accused of having a financial interest in the outcome. According to Kid McCoy who was in San Francisco fighting on the under card and witnessed the championship fight as he was considered a contender for the heavyweight championship in his memoirs he wrote;

> *"After the fight my manager and I along with Danny Lynch, Billy Needham, Bat Masterson and Wyatt Earp were all in a bar having a beer, although, Mr. Earp, as usual he was drinking a cup of coffee. We no more sat down at our table, when in came Bob Fitzsimmons and his manager. I don't think they realized we were sitting at a table in the back of the bar. Mr. Earp sat in the corner chair with his back to the wall, as they strolled up to the bar. He heard Fitzsimmons call him every bad word under the sun."*

Below is a cartoon that appeared in the New York Times on December 4, 1896 two days after the fight

"FITZ"   TOM"

THE "BAD MAN" REFEREE

Fitzsimmons and his manager went up to the bar and ordered a drink. Then Fitzsimmons was heard all through the bar making a statement, that if he ever saw Earp again that he would deck him for making such a bad call, that cost him the fight. Wyatt Earp stood up and calmly apologized stating;

> *"Excuse me gentleman, just for a minute, as, I need to address this right now. I will be back momentarily."*

Wyatt Earp got up and calmly walked up to the bar and moved in right next to Fitzsimmons. He tapped Bob on the back and said;

> *"I'm right here Bob, so stop talking and let's get it done right here and now."*

Then Wyatt calmly removed his gun and holster and placed them on the bar and said,

> *"There Bob, that's just so you know that this will be a fair fight."*

Then he looked right into Bob Fitzsimmons eyes and said boldly;

> *"I saw everything you have and I told you several times how to beat Sharkey but you continued to hit him with blows below the belt. I will let you make the first move and then I will personally take you out right here with two punches. It's your move Bob?"*

According to Kid McCoy in his memoirs, Bob Fitzsimmons looked right at Wyatt Earp, then calmly turned around and walked out of the bar. Then Wyatt Earp came back our table, smiled and said;

"I knew he was not going to do anything because he knew that I told him how to beat Sharkey and he knew damn well that he was hitting Sharkey with low blows. Besides, in his mind he had to be thinking that if I told him how to beat Sharkey that for sure I knew how to beat him. Needless to say, I was watching his hands, in case he started to make a move."

Below is a great cartoon that appeared in the San Francisco Examiner the day after the altercation that Wyatt Earp had with Bob Fitzsimmons in the Saloon.

THIS H'YAR RING AIN'T BIG 'NUFF FER THE TWO OF YA'.

DARYL CAGLE
Source:
Great Sporting Eccentrics;
Randall/Richardson Steirman & Black

cagle.com
©Daryl Cagle

Wyatt Earp *refereed an 1896 boxing match wearing two six shooters. He drew on one boxer, ordering him back to his corner and then turned his guns on the angry crowd.*

Chapter Nine

Below is the statement after the fight by W.W. Naughton, the well known sportswriter of that time period, who said as follows;

> *"The Earp decision in the Sharkey vs Fitzsimmons Championship fight is the greatest scandal of the modern boxing ring era."*

The fight was already a controversial event when the morning San Francisco papers hit the news-stands. It has become more so over the years as the third man in the ring assumed the stature of one of the leading controversial figures of the frontier west, rivaling Wild Bill Hickock and Billy the Kid in numbers of admirers and detractors.

The Sharkey-Fitzsimmons fight has become a point of contention in the seemingly endless controversy of Wyatt Earp. One point, however, is agreed upon by all parties involved in the controversy. Whether the fight was fixed or not, it took plenty of sheer nerve to do What Wyatt Earp did that night. The evidence strongly suggests fraud, and yet, on the basis of what was later revealed, if it was a fix it was certainly one of the most ambitious frauds ever perpetrated.

The morning after the fight found San Francisco and the sporting world at large abuzz with the news. Speculation was rampant. Two San Francisco newspapers, the Chronicle and the Call, were flatly of the opinion that Fitzsimmons had been robbed, while the Examiner's stand was somewhat equivocal. The Examiner and he Call were in the midst of a journalistic feud at that time, and the Call utilized the fact that Earp had written several accounts of his life on the frontier for the Examiner to link that paper to Earp. Wyatt Earp was characterized as the *"Bad Man Referee."* The Examiner and the Call used sensationalism, as the ensuring weeks were to prove, but whether it was simply yellow journalism or not, the San Francisco papers raised questions that needed to be answered. The initial coverage suggested the great controversy that was to follow.

Ned Foster, a very good friend of Bob Fitzsimmons, who was present at ringside and saw it all told a newspaper reporter;

> *"Although I am a friend of Fitz, I think he fouled Sharkey and therefore I have no fault to find with the decision. I know Wyatt Earp to be an honest man and a true sportsman."*

E.J. Baldwin, a well known San Francisco businessman who was also present at ringside and saw the fight told a reporter;

> *"Fitz fouled Sharkey in as vile a manner as I've ever witnessed."*

Captain I.W. Lees, Chief Detective of San Francisco's police department, who was also present at ringside and witnessed the whole fight reported;

> *"On two occasions during the fight, Mr. Earp went to Fitzsimmons corner to warn him and his manager that he was hitting below the belt and explained how Fitz could avoid further low blows and he also warned him that if he continued hitting Sharkey below the belt that he would be forced to stop the fight and*

award Sharkey the winner."

Contrary to the two witnesses statements above, W.C. Vreeland, a newspaper reporter also present at ringside, expressed a somewhat different and popular view when he said;

> *"I think the decision was outrageous."*

T.T. Williams, a sportswriter, was bewildered; pointing out that Fitz had no reason to foul. He spoke;

> *"For the first time in the history of the prize ring in California it was necessary to disarm the referee."*

When Earp was arrested for carrying a concealed weapon and released upon $50.00 bail, it became clear that there were those who did not feel so lightly about Earp's pistol-toting habit. The Call intimated that it was not by chance that the *"Arizona Bad Man"* was armed. Earp was believed to have carried a pistol in order to stand off the irate multitude that witnessed his brazen robbery of Fitzsimmons. Of course not even the *"hero of the O.K Corral"* would have been foolish enough to attempt to shoot his way out of Mechanic's Pavilion. But the story made good newspaper article, and some people appeared to believe it.

But there were more significant questions than why the redoubtable Wyatt Earp wore a revolver into the ring. Fitzsimmons and his manager were saying publicly and loudly that Fitz had been robbed, implicating not only Earp but Sharkey and his manager as well to be in on a fix. Moreover, Fitzsimmons added;

"No pugilist can get a square deal from the thieves who handle fighting in this city and it is a safe bet that the last big fight San Francisco will ever see was pulled off tonight."

Wyatt Earp reportedly called the accusations as *"rubbish,"* and the Examiner published a statement supposedly made by Earp;

"I have met Bob Fitzsimmons several times over the years, the first, I believe, being four or five years ago, when one of my best friends I have in the country and one of the truest supporters Fitzsimmons ever had, Bat Masterson, introduced us in Denver. I am very sure that Bat Masterson has lost a great deal of money on this fight, but I have always been able to decide what is right even against my own pay. My friends can stand the consequences of such a decision."

"I feel that I did the right and honorable thing. Feeling so, I care nothing for the opinion of anybody. I saw the foul blow struck as plainly as I see you. That is all there is to the story. No man until now has ever questioned my honor. I have been in many places and peculiar situations, but no one ever said, until tonight, that I was guilty of a dishonorable act."

Julian worked rapidly, apparently unimpressed by the purported spotlessness of Wyatt Earp's honesty. By the time Lynch, Sharkey's manager in company of Earp, arrived at the First National Bank to cash the check, they found an injunction had been issued by a judge in the judicial system, had been issued preventing payment to Sharkey the winner, until a thorough investigation could be made. Julian was challenging the entire fight game in California and Fitzsimmons threat seemed rather ominous.

The loss in the fight, seemed to have been the only basis of Julian's action, nothing should probably have come from the incident. But it was clear from the start that Julian meant to follow up on his ringside objection to Wyatt Earp as referee, and Earp's decision in the ring just fueled his anger.

Contrary to popular belief, the referee was named publicly before noon on the day of the fight, rather than at the ring. Julian reported that at about two o'clock on the afternoon before the fight, Riley Grannan, Tom James, well known local gamblers, and M.A. Gunst, police commissioner, sought out Julian in the Baldwin Hotel. According to the story, Julian had just learned the name of the referee from a bartender in the hotel. Riley Grannan spoke for the little delegation.

Grannan told Julian that he had been trying to bet on Fitzsimmons but could find no takers. At one of the local race tracks, Grannan went on that he saw Earp talking to another gambler named Joe Harvey. Grannan reported hearing Harvey say to Earp;

"Well it's all right now, is it?"

To which he heard Earp reply;
"You can count on me."

After this, Grannan said that he had no difficulty in placing his bets. Moreover, he asserted, the word moved rapidly among sporting men that Sharkey was set to win the match. At that point M.A. Gunst the other gambler with them interjected;

> *"How in the name of heaven did you ever agree to have a man with the reputation and standing of this fellow Wyatt Earp selected as the referee?"*

Julian explained that he and Lynch could not agree on a third man in the ring, and that J.J. Groom and J.D. Gibbs of the National Club selected Wyatt Earp to be the referee.

Later that afternoon Julian encountered Wyatt Earp, and, according to Julian, told him what he had heard. He then asked Earp to step down. By Julian's account, Earp refused, saying that he had been chosen and would not withdraw unless asked to do so by the National Club. With that Earp turned on his heel and left. Wyatt Earp's version of the encounter varied in detail. He said that when he was approached by Fitzsimmons manager, he assured Julian that the charges were false, after which Julian left, apparently satisfied with Earp's guarantee of an honest fight.

After the fight Julian was also asking serious questions about Sharkey. Why had the National Club doctor, D.D. Lusting, been turned away from Sharkey's dressing room? He was unimpressed by the announcement of Doctor B.B. Lee, that Sharkey had suffered a blow to the groin which had left him confined to bed in great pain. Even after Lynch explained that he had not admitted the club doctor because he was angry with the club officials for allowing the pre-fight haggle, Julian remained unmoved.

On December 4, 1896, two days after the fight, seven doctors examined Sharkey and they filed the following report;

> "We find an edema, or swelling on the right side, of his privates extending partially to the left side, also two small spots, discolorations, or bruises about one-half way down the inside of his right upper thigh."

Below is an illustration from a reporter present in the room, of the doctors gathering at the bedside of boxer Tom Sharkey a day after Sharkey had to leave the fight because of an injury. No photos were allowed to be taken in Sharkey's hospital room.

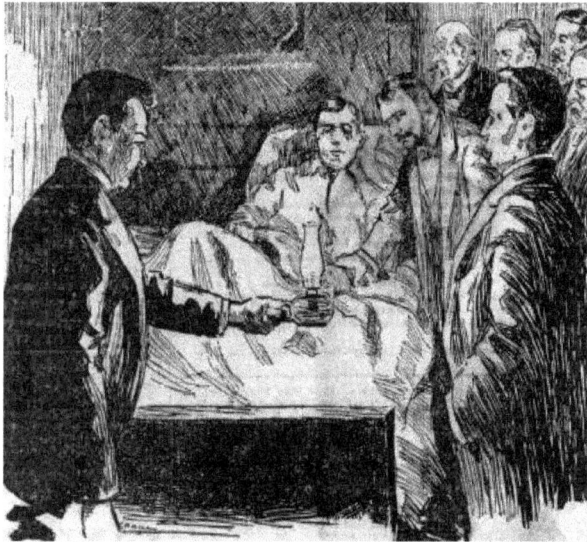

The doctors concluded that at least one serious blow to the groin was received by Sharkey in the fight and that he was not able to continue to fight with such an injury. However, one of the examining physicians vigorously dissented from the majority report, asserting that the injury might have been caused by something else other than a blow to his groin. In any case he felt the blow was not severe enough to cause the kind of pain necessary to put Sharkey out of the fight. Julian accepted the latter view.

J.D. Gibbs, a known local gambler at ringside gave his version, that appeared in the San Francisco Examiner on December 7, 1896;

> *"Wyatt Earp was very highly recommended to us. I did not know him personally, but, like every other sporting main in the United States, I definitely heard of him. Whatever else may be said of Wyatt Earp, he enjoys the reputation of being one of the squarest sporting man in America. I had never heard even an insinuation against his honor. On that score at least we felt reasonably sure, as to his qualifications as a referee Earp himself told me that he had acted in such capacity in over thirty fights.*
>
> *I say that if there was anything wrong about that match, or with the referee or with anyone connected with it, I want the whole matter exposed. The club's reputation is at stake and my personal reputation as well. I will say openly and publicly that I knew nothing that would tend to show that the contest was not absolutely on the square.*
>
> *A week ago last Sunday I joined a party of gentlemen who had arranged a trip to nearby Sausalito, California, their object being to visit Bob Fitzsimmons at his training headquarters, but I did not know him. I had often heard of him, but*

had never seen him before. It was not until we were returning on the boat from Sausalito, however, that I met Wyatt Earp. Billy Jordan, who was the master of ceremonies at Mechanics Pavilion, introduced us. We all sat down and chatted about Fitzsimmons' conditioning, then about boxing contests in general.

It was during this talk that Jordan said something about Mr. Earp having served as referee in many good contests. I asked Mr. Earp about his referee background and he told me that he had refereed over thirty professional boxing matches.

Later that day I told my associate, Mr. Groom, that I had found a man who would fill the bill in our big match in the event that Sharkey and Fitzsimmons failed to decide on a man to referee the fight. When I mentioned Wyatt Earp's name, he agreed that he was just the man for the job. Nothing more was said about the matter for a week. We did note even tell Mr. Earp that we were thinking of asking him to serve. We did not even know if he would accept the offer if it was given to him. During this intervening week Mr. Groom prepared a list of eligible local referees. But we forgot to include Wyatt Earp's name when we presented the list to the respective managers of Sharkey and Fitzsimmons as well as the National Club fight chairmen. After the first unsuccessful conference, it was found *that every man named had been rejected by all the parties.*

By this time it was practically settled that the managers were not going to agree on a referee, so Groom and I had a consultation at the Baldwin Hotel. We decided to ask Mr. Earp to serve. We took him into a private room in San Francisco Police Commissioners office ad laid the matter before him. Mr. Earp first refused. He said he was not seeking notoriety and would far rather watch the contest from a spectator's seat. But after an hour of coaxing him we finally got him to consent.

Now, Mr. Julian the manager of Fitzsimmons and Mr. Lynch, the manager of Sharkey were approached and both hailed the selection of Wyatt Earp as referee with great satisfaction. Everybody we told about the decision to have Mr. Earp referee the fight said we could not have chosen a better man for the job. When the San Francisco Examiner printed the story that Wyatt Earp had been chosen to referee the fight, we received congratulations from all sides.

It was not until I went to Fitzsimmons' dressing room that night just before the fight was to begin to tell them to prepare to go into the ring, that I heard of any objection to the choosing of Wyatt Earp as the referee. Julian and Fitzsimmons both said they had heard that the fight had been fixed. I was thunderstruck. Well, to make a long story short, they went into the ring and that long wrangle with which everybody is familiar with that took place. While they were talking Earp came to me and begged to be allowed to retire. But by this time I had become somewhat worked up over the actions of Julian and Fitzsimmons, believing as I did that they were not sincere, and I made Earp promise to stand his ground. Under the articles of the agreement with the club, that had the privilege of selecting the referee in the event the principals could not agree on a suitable man, and at that late stage of the proceedings, I proposed to stand by our selection. The spectators were becoming impatient, and the delay was irritating.

That is the entire story of how Wyatt Earp happened to be selected as the referee, and I hope it will dispel any idea that there has been any collusion or robbery."

It was an excellent article, but neither Julian nor the San Francisco Call Newspaper accepted it, that should not be a surprise, since the Call was owned by Julian. The Call informed its readers that Mr. Earp had been suggested to the National Athletic Club by Andrew Lawrence, editor of the Examiner, who both called by the enterprising writers of the Call, *"Long Green,"* were actually supposedly pulling the strings in the fraud. And furthermore, J.J. Groom, supposedly now, apparently says that he was not as enthusiastic about Mr. Earp as his partner, confirmed the Call's accusation, but he was fine before the fight. The San Francisco Call and

Julian were able to keep the controversy alive by fresh accusations and the new twist to the story, as usual Wyatt Earp remained silent.

Wyatt Earp having had more of his share of difficulties in his lifetime, was not been in very good financial condition for some time prior to the fight, which suggests the reason he may have conspired to fix the fight but, when he testified at the hearing later, that he owned a string of race horses in the San Francisco area, but upon close examination, he admitted the horses were merely leased from a Mrs. Orcher of Santa Rosa, California. Under the circumstances, the money he was promised for refereeing the fight would have come in handy, however it must be noted that Mr. Earp, in the past always thought in big terms.

After the fight, Earp was not only arrested, but his check for refereeing the fight was held up, pending the outcome of the hearing. Moreover, the newspapers seemed to delight in reminding him and others of his nefarious past. The Call had a heyday digging up embarrassing incidents in his life that Mr. Earp had to explain.

Almost immediately after the fight, Judge J.G. Swinnerton threatened Wyatt Earp with a lawsuit to recover the fees, he had put up as security in another matter about a year before. The lawsuit stated that three con men were arrested for swindling a farmer out of $2,000 in the old game of the tin box and rocks. Swinnerton was a practicing local attorney at that time. Mr. Earp said he would provide security, but at the time of the Sharkey-Fitzsimmons fight, he had not yet paid the money he owed Swinnerton. Earp planned to bet on the fight and make enough money to pay off his debt to Swinnerton. The case went to the courts shortly afterward and Judge Swinnerton attached two race horses owned by Earp in lieu of the $170.45 for legal services rendered.

On December 8, 1896, another case was filed asking a judgment of $2,121.21 as the result of the failure of Wyatt Earp and Marshall Williams to repay notes secured by them on October 29, 1881, following the O.K. Corral incident in Tombstone, Arizona Territory. The notes were in the amounts of $570.74 and $600, and were utilized as bail in Earp's legal defense, in the hearing that followed the death of the three cowboys, killed by the Earp faction at the Gunfight at the O.K. Corral.

Wyatt Earp's also had to attend a hearing for the charge of carrying a concealed weapon in the city of San Francisco, since he was caught wearing his holstered pistol, when he entered the ring on the evening of the fight that was held on December 4, 1896. At the hearing Mr. Earp explained that he carried a revolver to protect himself from the many enemies he had sent to prison, while he was a lawman on the frontier. The judge was not impressed and fined Earp $50.

The following day, the San Francisco Call accused Earp of attempting to fix a horse race in San Diego, California on May 5, 1890. According to the story, Mr. Earp sized up the race and then approached the owner of the favored horse and asked him to throw the race for a sizeable sum. The owner of the horse, Harvey McCarthy, refused because a large group of Mexican Citizen's had bet on his horse to win. Earp had already informed the American gamblers of his intentions and was unable to tell them of McCarthy's refusal to go along with the fix. When McCarthy's horse won the race, the irate Anglos produced knives, guns and a rope to take care of Earp for double crossing them. The real irony was that it was McCarthy, who just happened to be a deputy ·sheriff who protected Wyatt Earp from the lynch mob set to take their vengeance for what, they believed was a double cross. Whether the story was true or not, the publicity did not help Earp's reputation.

Nor did the following article that appeared in the Call the same day helped his reputation;

> *"Wyatt Earp, his brother's James and Warren along with other followers still stand indicted for the murder of Frank Stilwell in Tucson, Arizona Territory on March 20, 1882. The indictment has never been squashed and the Earp's and their friends are still wanted for crimes committed in Tombstone October 19, 1881 through the end of the year 1882."*

To make matters worse, writers like Alfred Henry Lewis took advantage of Wyatt Earp's sudden prominence to write thrilling, not well researched, accounts of Earp's adventures in Tombstone and Dodge City.

It was a matter of fact that Earp's frontier background was the main reason he was chosen to be the referee. However, Wyatt and Josie Earp's long stay in California and Arizona, had not been without event. Described by the Call as the thorn in the side of the former Chief of Police in Tombstone, David Neagle with whom Earp, had several encounters while living in Tombstone. It was reported that Neagle was willing to take on Wyatt Earp after the Sharkey-Fitzsimmons fight.

Armed with tales of the Tombstone Territory, Wyatt Earp, the Examiner explained was why Wyatt Earp was chosen as the referee;

> *"This man was considered not one to be intimidated by either fighter or by public clamor. As a consequence his choice by the National Athletic Club met with general approval."*

The outcome proved that, Mr. Earp was not easily intimidated, although his nerve's of steel in facing the crowd and the manager of Bob Fitzsimmons, Earp seemed to reflect more of an economic motive rather than scrupulous honesty. Wyatt Earp moved through the entire supposed fixed fight affair with a nonchalant manner, which is truly remarkable. But not really surprising since he dealt with so many nasty, bad characters as a deputy marshal in Dodge City and Tombstone, he just seemed not the least bit affected by the public clamor and resentment. Wyatt Earp was the kind of man, who could bluff or bull his way through almost any situation, a trait that followed him his whole life.

While Wyatt Earp's troubles were mounting the hearing was proceeding rapidly. Martin Julian had secured the testimony of two of Sharkey's seconds, Billy Smith and George Allen. Smith, who had been involved in a shady fight with *"Brooklyn Jimmy"* Carroll, was the first to testify. He asserted that Wyatt Earp *"threw"* the fight Sharkey's way for $2,500 promised him by Danny Lynch. Moreover, he testified that Sharkey and Lynch were partners in the National Athletic Club with Gibbs and Groom. He attributed the choice of Wyatt Earp to Lynch, Sharkey's manager, who had known Earp through his horse racing activities;

"Sharkey told Billy Smith that Lynch knew a race horse man by the name of Wyatt Earp. Tom could not pronounce his name right but I definitely knew who he meant."

Billy Smith swore that Tom Sharkey was not hurt, except for a cauliflower ear, and that Sharkey received instructions from Lynch about how he should act in the ring. He swore that Lynch had tried to obtain the services of Hiram Cook who refused to go along with the scheme to rob Fitzsimmons. Cook later denied that Lynch had approached him.

George Allen's testimony corroborated that of Smith, but in cross-examination both witnesses fared badly. General Barnes, the defense attorney, battered their testimony unmercifully until both witnesses were virtually discredited. Cook and Allen had argued with Lynch regarding money after the fight.

These surprise witnesses were followed by Fitzsimmons, Julian, Sharkey and Lynch, all of whom repeated that they had already related to the newspapers.

Below is a copy of the first published newspaper article that appeared in the New York Times on December 5, 1896 about the disputed decision;

The   Fitzsimmons-Sharkey   fight Dispute

SAN FRANCISCO, Dec 4- The purse of $10,000 has not been paid to Sharkey yet. The courts will have to settle who is entitled to the money. Physicians are not agreed as to whether

112

Sharkey was disabled by a foul or not. Sporting men are having heated controversies about the matter. And opinion is divided as to the facts.

Below is another article about the fight, that appeared in the San Francisco Examiner on December 8, 1896 six days after the match.

FITZSIMMONS ROBBED

San Francisco December 8- Fitzsimmons' fighting all through the match was in marked contrast of that of Sharkey. Bob broke away promptly from clinches and made no attempt to strike. The New Zealander showed himself a master of his craft. He cunningly kept away from the sailor's mad rushes, poking his long left into Sharkey's face whenever he got too near. Sharkey could get inside of that long, thin arm, which, when he was standing straight up, was like a bar of steel. It was a lively fight from the start. Bob was more aggressive than Sharkey and kept his man on the move all the time.

In the first round Fitz saw an opening and a right swing to the jaw sent Sharkey to the floor. That made the sailor a bit cautious and during the next four rounds he tried to keep out of the reach of the taller Fitzsimmons. In the fourth round Sharkey pushed Fitz over on the floor and before Fitz could get up, made a couple of vicious swipes at him. Fitz cleverly clinched and avoided damage, but it was a clear case of foul on Sharkey's part. No claim was made however, and the fight continued.

After supposedly being fouled in the eighth round and made unconscious Sharkey recovered about a half hour after being taken to his dressing room, he was apparently badly injure, his groin being swollen after the doctors did their initial diagnosis. Sharkey says he had Bob Fitzsimmons going until the eighth round before the foul occurred. Wyatt Earp, again the referee, says the foul was deliberate. Bob Fitzsimmons, just before striking his left hook that apparently knocked Sharkey out, hit the sailor below the belt with his fist. Earlier in the fight in a breakaway, Referee Wyatt Earp says Fitzsimmons deliberately struck Sharkey over the eye with his elbow, creating a large cut. Earp was tempted to give Sharkey the fight in an earlier round when Fitz fouled him the first time, then and there, but the sailor made not claim and he allowed the contest to proceed.

It is estimated that the National Club took in at least $40,000 at the box office. At 9 o'clock, before three quarters of the seats were filled, the preliminaries were called and a number of local celebrities exhibited their prowess. Harry Stafford of New Orleans and John Howard of San Francisco had Fitz ahead on their cards when the fight ended in the eighth round.

The following is another article that was published in the New York Times on December 9, 1896, regarding the fight and the outcome;

SAYS THE FIGHT WAS "FIXED."

Sharkey's Trainer Tells of alleged Conspiracy

SAN FRANCISCO, Dec. 9- A large assembly of ring followers and men about town crowded Judge Sanderson's courtroom this morning expecting to hear the sensational developments regarding the manner in which the Fitzsimmons-Sharkey Heavy Weight Championship prizefight that was "fixed," and they were not disappointed.

If credence is to placed in the story told on the witness stand by Sharkey's trainer, "Austrailian" Billy Smith, Bob Fitzsimmons was a defeated man before he left New York. According to Smith's testimony, J.J. Groom, J.H. Gibbs, Danny Lynch, Sharkey's manager, and Sharkey himself were the men who composed the National Athletic Club, before which organization the contest was fought. These four men, Smith swears, engaged Wyatt Earp as referee, with the understanding that he was to award Sharkey the fight directly after Fitzsimmons landed a body blow or stomach punch, which might be stretched into a foul. Earp was to receive $2,500 for his services.

On December 10, 1896, referee Wyatt Earp took the witness stand. In a quiet, steady voice he calmly called Martin Julian and Bob Fitzsimmons liars. He swore that his honor had never been questioned and practically challenged Julian to prove his charges. Wyatt Earp's demeanor was quiet and cool as well as quite startling to those in attendance. Colonel Kowalsky in attendance accused Wyatt Earp of coming into the courtroom armed. Earp smiled beneath his handle bar moustache, but his eyes were cold. He denied the charge, challenging the lawyer to have Wyatt Earp searched. Kowalsky decided to accept Mr. Earp's word.

The following article that pertains to this fight was published in the New York Times on December 18, 1896 and sheds more light on the payoffs.

SHARKEY GETS $8,500

> *San Francisco December 18- As soon as the Anglo-Californian Bank opened this morning, "Tom" Sharkey presented the certified check for $10,000 handed him by Wyatt Earp on the day of the fight with Fitzsimmons. The cashier notified the sailor that attachments aggregating $1,500 had been filed against the certificate. "All right; then give me the balance," remarked Sharkey, in a way which indicated that he was anxious to get the $8,500 balance of the proceeds out of reach of potential collectors. The money was turned over to him, and he proceeded on his way jubilantly.*

Chapter Ten

With the new twist to the story, Martin Julian was able to obtain a hearing to get the facts to determine exactly what had actually happened surrounding the fact that the fight may have been fixed. The actual hearing got under way on December 4, 1896. Julian retained Colonel H.I. Kowalski, a well-known and well respected San Francisco attorney, while Lynch obtained the services of another well known lawyer retired General W.H.L. Barnes. A number of witnesses were subpoenaed, among them Wyatt Earp, who was threatened with arrest when he failed to appear in court on the opening day

Wyatt Earp was having more than his share of difficulties. During his testimony, Wyatt Earp admitted that his record as a professional referee had been a little stretched. Instead of refereeing twenty to thirty professional boxing matches of which Gibbs spoke, he actually had only one professional job as a referee and that was recently in San Diego. However he went on to state for the record that he had refereed eighteen to thirty bare knuckle fights in Mexico and across the west. Moreover, Earp denied having made any statements to the newspapers, thereby denying the authenticity of the Examiner article

All of the witnesses having been heard and several days of haggling having ensured, General Barnes, on December 16, 1896, made a motion for dissolving the injunction against payment of the check on the basis that the boxing match was a prize fight and therefore illegal under the laws of California. The counsel for Fitz objected strongly, maintaining that the event in question was not a *"prize fight"* but a *"golden glove contest."*

It was on this basis of this difference that boxing had continued in California after the anti-prize fight law was passed. After the Sharkey-Fitzsimmons fight there appeared in California a strong movement to outlaw boxing altogether. After hearing the arguments of counsel, Judge Sanderson took the question under advisement until the next day when the court would reconvene.

When the court reconvened the following morning, Judge Sanderson threw out the injunction on the basis that it was in violation of the anti-prize fight legislation of California. He reminded Sharkey, Fitzsimmons, and all of the other involved parties that they were amendable to indictment, for their participation in a prize fight. Action has never taken. Sharkey cashed his check and Wyatt Earp was paid for refereeing the fight. Julian and Fitz continued to maintain that they had been robbed.

Thus, officially, ended the Sharkey-Fitzsimmons controversy, absolutely nothing had been solved. The hearing only proved that ninety per cent of the witnesses were champion liars. The questions raised were still unanswered. In the eyes of the law the fight had been illegal, and, subsequently, it was of no importance to ascertain what really happened, even if the facts could have been determined.

The mystery surrounding the fix of the Sharkey-Fitzsimmons Heavyweight Championship fight on the night of December 2, 1896 remains unsolved after over the hundred years that have passed since that fateful night. Most of the attempts to unravel the facts surrounding the possible "fix" have met with little success. Everyone suspects it was a "fix," but boxing "fixes" are notoriously difficult to uncover. Even assuming that the fight was a fraud, the question of responsibility has never been placed.

Martin Julian's story actually has the fewest loopholes. His charges of collusion between Wyatt Earp and the National Club, including Sharkey and Lynch, may be the answer. Still Julian's story is too pat. Julian knew too much. Either he was a detective of the first rank, or he created the story to keep the controversy from dying with his man, the defeated fighter. It was very difficult to cast Martin Julian as a hero.

Several years ago another writer, Stewart Lake, who wrote in his book, Wyatt Earp Frontier Marshall giving a different and perhaps a more clearly correct version of the affair. It was supposed to have been related to him by Wyatt Earp's lifelong best friend and lawman himself, Bat Masterson, but when approached later, Masterson denied giving this account. Masterson was not a man who divulged information about his friends. It was recorded when Bat Masterson was working for the New York Morning Telegraph newspaper as a sports reporter, the entire affair was the work of Earp and Julian, Fitzsimmons' manager with Fitzsimmons, Sharkey nor Lynch, who was Sharkey's manager, had any knowledge of the plot to fix the fight.

On the strength of Wyatt Earp's presence in the ring, Martin Julian placed a $10,000 bet on Sharkey at the three to one odds favoring Fitzsimmons. Thus when Sharkey won on a foul and was awarded the prize money, the $30,000 won on the bet was divided equally among Earp, Julian and Fitzsimmons, that made the loser's winnings considerably more than the winner's take for the fight.

It's an interesting story, but one not without its faults. His story is intriguing and probably came directly from Wyatt Earp. But Bat Masterson was not above spinning a yarn at times. The basic problem with Masterson's supposed story is that it does not take into account a number of significant factors. Some of these additional factors can, however, be easily placed into the basic framework which his story affords.

For example, it explains the relative silence of Sharkey and Lynch, scapegoats of the Masterson account. The pre fight haggle, which has all the earmarks of a staged performance, adequately removed Julian from suspicion. Even the attempts to implicate the National Athletic Club do not conflict with Masterson's story. What is suggested here is merely that the fraud was more highly organized than Masterson's story indicates.

But there are more direct problems. If Earp was Julian's partner in such a scheme why did Julian try so hard to discredit Earp, it would, of course, remove suspicion from him, but the effect on Earp was hardly advantageous. Whatever else Earp was, he was definitely no fool. In light of the Masterson story, which is very doubtful, since he and Wyatt Earp were such close friends, it is all the more amazing that Earp made no effort to defend himself during the public controversy, except to the hearing where his statements were simple and reserved.

A more basic difficulty with the Masterson account is Sharkey. Insofar as we know, this fighter was not an actor. However, if we accept the Masterson version, then Sharkey did not know he was suppose to be fouled. Yet, when he went down clutching at his groin, the news commentators were in agreement that Sharkey appeared to be in great pain, which in fact made him become unconscious. These facts along with the attending physicians report make it extremely difficult to explain why Sharkey, if he was not involved, reacted as he did, and where, if not in a fight, was he the recipient of such incredible the edema in his groin.

At this point it is important to the reader, the author present a history of Bat Masterson, a life long best friend of the Earp family but especially Wyatt Earp, since his loyalty to Earp is being discussed.

William Barclay "Bat" Masterson (November 26, 1853 – October 25, 1921) was a figure of the American Old West known as a buffalo hunter, U.S. Marshal and Army scout, avid fisherman, gambler, frontier lawman, and sports editor and columnist for the *New York Morning Telegraph*. He was the brother of lawmen James Masterson and Ed Masterson.

Born on November 26, 1853, at Henryville, Canada East, in the Eastern Townships of what is Quebec today, and baptized as Bartholomew Masterson, he later used the name "William Barclay Masterson".

His father, Thomas Masterson (*or Mastersan*), was born in Canada, of an Irish family; and his mother, Catherine McGurk (*or McGureth*), was born in Ireland. He was the second child in a family of five brothers and two sisters. They were raised on farms in Quebec, New York, and Illinois, until they finally settled near Wichita, Kansas.

In his late teens, he and two of his brothers, Ed Masterson and James Masterson, left their family's farm to become buffalo hunters. While traveling without his brothers, Bat took part in the Battle of Adobe Walls in Texas and killed Comanche

Indians. He then spent time as a U.S. Army scout in a campaign against the Kiowa and Comanche Indians.

Bat Masterson's first gunfight took place in 1876 in Sweetwater, Texas, *(later called Mobeetie, Wheeler County, Texas)* not to be confused with the current Sweetwater, the seat of Nolan County west of Abilene, Texas. He was attacked by a soldier, Corporal Melvin A. King, in a fight, allegedly because of a girl. The girl, Mollie Brennan, stopped one of King's bullets and was killed. King, whose real name was Anthony Cook, died of his wounds. Masterson was shot in the pelvis, but recovered.

In 1877, he joined his brothers in Dodge City, Kansas. Jim was the partner of Ed who was an assistant marshal. Soon after his arrival, Masterson came into conflict with the local marshal over the treatment of a man being arrested. He was jailed and fined, although his fine was later returned by the city council. He served as a sheriff's deputy alongside Wyatt Earp, and within a few months, Masterson was elected county sheriff of Ford County, Kansas. As sheriff, Bat won plaudits for capturing four members of the Mike Roark gang who had unsuccessfully held up a train at nearby Kinsley. He also led the posse that captured Jim Kennedy who had inadvertently killed an entertainer named Dora Hand in Dodge.

Fighting in Colorado on the Santa Fe side of its war against the Rio Grande railroad, Masterson continued as Ford County sheriff until he was voted out of office in 1879. During this same period his brother Ed was Marshal of Dodge City and died in the line of duty on April 9, 1878. Ed was shot by a cowboy named Jack Wagner who was unaware that Bat was in the vicinity. As Ed stumbled away from the scene, Masterson responded from across the street with deadly force, firing on both Wagner and Wagner's boss, Alf Walker. Wagner died the next day but Walker was taken back to Texas and recovered. The local newspapers were ambiguous about who shot Wagner and Walker and this led some later historians to question whether Bat was involved. However, the recent location of two court cases in which Bat testified under oath that he had shot both means that most now accept that Bat avenged his brother.

For the next several years, Bat Masterson made a living as a gambler moving through several of the legendary towns of the Old West. Wyatt Earp invited Masterson to Tombstone, Arizona Territory, in early 1881 where Earp owned a one-quarter interest in the gambling concession at the Oriental Saloon in exchange for his services as a manager and enforcer. He wanted his help running the faro tables in the Oriental Saloon. Bat remained until April 1881, when Bat received an unsigned telegram that compelled him to immediately return to Dodge City.

Jim Masterson was in partnership with A. J. Peacock in Dodge City's Lady Gay Saloon and Dance Hall. Al Updegraff was Peacock's brother-in-law and bartender. Jim thought Updegraff was dishonest and a drunk, and demanded that Peacock fire Updegraff, which Peacock refused to do. Their disagreement grew until threats flew, at which time Bat received the telegram indicating his brothers life was in danger. Masterson jumped on the next stage out of Tombstone and arrived in Dodge City on April 16. Jumping off the train before it stopped, Masterson saw Updegraff and Peacock. He accosted them;

"Hold up there a minute, you two. I want to talk to you."

Recognizing Bat, the two retreated behind the jail, and the three began exchanging gunfire. Citizens ran for cover as bullets ripped through the Long Branch Saloon. Other individuals began firing in support of both sides until Updegraff was shot. Mayor Abe Webster arrested Masterson and only then did he learn that his brother Jim was fine. Updegraff slowly recovered, and since it could not be determined who shot Updegraff, Masterson was fined $8.00 and released.

Bat was known as a gunman and an excellent shot. If he fired first and without warning, as Updegraff and Peacock claimed, it was extremely unlikely he would have missed. Updegraff and Peacock did not explain why they were headed towards the train depot, guns under their coats. The citizens were outraged, warrants were issued, but Bat and Jim were permitted to leave Dodge.

Masterson spent a year as marshal of Trinidad, Colorado as well as serving as Sheriff of South Pueblo, Colorado. In 1883, he participated in a bloodless conflict and gunfighter gathering later called the Dodge City War.

In 1888 Masterson was living in Denver, Colorado, where he dealt faro for *"Big Ed"* Chase at the Arcade gambling house. In 1888 he managed and then purchased the Palace Variety Theater. It was probably there that Bat first met an Indian club swinger and singer called Emma Moulton, born as Emma Walter near Philadelphia in 1857. The pair subsequently lived together and it has been widely reported that they married in Denver on 21 November 1891. Although no record of the marriage has come to light thus far and Emma was not divorced from her first husband until 9 November 1893, the partnership was to survive until Bat's death. While living in Denver, he met and maintained a long term friendship with the infamous confidence man, Soapy Smith and members of the Soap Gang.

In 1889 the two friends were involved together in the famous Denver registration and election fraud scandal. In 1892 he moved to the silver boom town of Creede, Colorado, where he managed the Denver Exchange Club until the town was destroyed by fire. On the 1900 Federal Census record for Arapahoe County in Denver he lists his name as William Masterson with his birthplace as Missouri in 1854. His wife is listed as Emma Masterson married for 10 years and he lists his occupation as Athletic Club Keeper. Bat continued to travel around the boom towns of the West, gambling and promoting prize fights. He began writing a weekly sports column for *George's Weekly,* a Denver newspaper, and opened the Olympic Athletic Club to promote the sport of boxing.

Bat Masterson lived in the American West during a violent and frequently lawless period. His most recent biographer concluded that, Indian-fighting aside; he used a firearm against a fellow man on just six occasions, far less than some of his contemporaries such as *Dallas Stoudenmire, "Wild Bill"* Hickok, and *Clay Allison.* However, the fact that he was so widely known as a gunfighter can be described as a practical joke played on a gullible newspaper reporter in August 1881. Seeking a copy in Gunnison, Colorado, the reporter asked Dr W.S. Cockrell about man killers. Dr. Cockrell pointed to a young man nearby and said it was Bat Masterson and said that he had killed 26 men. Cockrell then regaled the reporter with several lurid tales about Bat's exploits and the reporter wrote them up for the *New York Sun*. The story was then widely reprinted in papers all over the country and became the basis for many more exaggerated stories told about Bat Masterson over the years. Masterson left the West and went to New York City by 1902, where he was arrested for illegal gambling.

President Theodore Roosevelt, on the recommendation of mutual friend Alfred Henry Lewis, appointed Masterson to the position of deputy to U.S. Marshal for the southern district of New York, under William Henkel. Roosevelt had met Masterson on several occasions and had become friendly with him. Masterson split his time between his writing and keeping the peace in the grand jury room whenever the U. S. Attorney in New York held session. He performed this service for about $2,000 per year from early 1908 until 1912 when President William Howard Taft removed Masterson from the position during Taft's purge of Roosevelt supporters from government positions. Bat Masterson worked as a sports writer and editor; and a columnist. His career as a writer started around 1883 and ended at his death in New York City in 1921.

Bat Masterson wrote a letter published in the *Daily Kansas State Journal*, on June 9, 1883, that mentioned his arrival in Dodge City, the famous Long Branch saloon, and his famous cohorts who made the Long Branch their headquarters during the so-called *"Dodge City Saloon War."* It was during this time that Bat met newspapermen Alfred Henry and William Eugene Lewis. Both journalists were destined to play a role in Masterson's future as a newspaper reporter. Masterson published *Vox Populi*, a single edition newspaper focusing on local Dodge City politics in November 1884. Masterson penned a weekly sports column for *George's Weekly* sometime after his arrival in Denver, Colorado, in the late 1890s.

Masterson continued his writing career in New York at the New York Morning Telegraph. A paper dedicated to sporting events, that featured the racing forms and results, and whose reputation was part of what was known as *"a whore's breakfast,"* that consisted of a cigarette and the morning telegraph. In 1904 he was hired by the younger Lewis brother, William Eugene Lewis, who also had a role as sports writer. Masterson later became the paper's sports editor. New York's politics, sporting events, theaters, fine dining establishments, and the great night life of his adopted city, became a way of life for him in his weekly column *"Masterson's Views on Timely Topics"* for more than 18 years. Lewis became the general manager and president of the paper and promoted his friend Masterson to company vice president/secretary.

While living in New York City, Bat Masterson became good friends of the Lewis brothers. W.E. Lewis eventually wrote several short stories and a novel called, *The Sunset Trail*, that was about Masterson. Alfred Lewis another of the Lewis brothers encouraged Bat to write a series of sketches about his adventures which were published by Lewis in the magazine he was an editor called Human Life (1904-1908). Masterson entertained his readers with stories about his days on the frontier and his gunfighter friends. He also explained to his readers what he felt were the best properties of a gunfighter.

It was during this time that Masterson sold his famous six-gun, *"the gun that tamed the West,"* because he needed the money. Actually, Masterson bought old guns at pawnshops, carved notches into the handles and sold them at inflated prices. Each time he claimed the gun was the one he used during his career as a lawman.

Bat Masterson died at age 67 on October 25, 1921, at his desk while living and working in New York City. He collapsed at his desk from a heart attack after penning what became his final column for the New York Morning Telegraph. His body was taken to Campbell's Funeral Parlor and later buried simple service in Woodlawn Cemetery in Bronx, New York. His full name appears on the headstone, William Barclay Masterson and above his epitaph on the large granite grave marker in Woodlawn. His epitaph states that he was *"Loved by everyone."*

Both of the photos below of **Bat** Masterson were found in our National Archives and are public domain.

Bat Masterson 1880   Bat Masterson 1920

128

The only significant contribution made about a possible fix was Masterson's supposed statement that he told to another reporter about the fight fix event was the implication of Martin Julian. Beyond that point speculation assumes control once more. It is highly probable though that the fix was a grand hoax involving everyone, who was a party to the fight. It is also possible that Lynch, finding himself a scapegoat, formulated a counterplot, bribing six doctors. But this does not explain Tom Sharkey's movement in the ring and the bruising of his inner thigh and groin. The doctors were selected by the participants in the fight and the National Athletic Club. If Masterson was correct in implicating Julian, each of the parties selecting doctors would have profited by such a report as the doctors turned in to the newspapers. Thus it is probable that the report was false. Sharkey's action's in the ring is the major problem left to be explained.

Famous Bat Masterson Quotations

"Every dog, we are told, has his day, unless there are more dogs than days."

"New York is the biggest boomtown there is. They will buy any damned thing here."

"When a man is at the racetrack he roars longer and louder over the twenty-five cents he loses through the hole in the bottom of his pocket than he does over the $25 he loses through the hole in the top of his pocket."

Below and following on the next page are the last recorded words that were found to be part of his column and were found on the typewriter

Masterson was using before he died while typing the quote;

> *"There are those who argue that everything breaks even in this old dump of a world of ours. I suppose these ginks who argue that way hold that because the rich man gets ice in the summer and the poor man gets it in the winter things are breaking even for both. Maybe so, but I'll swear I can't see it that way."*

It is a highly probability that Tom "Sailor" Sharkey was fouled, either as a part of the scheme or as a happy accident for the two fighters. The reporters perched high above the ring did not get a good view of the questionable blow, while at least half dozen reputable citizens near the ring swore that they saw the low blow very clearly. The mere fact that a foul was struck would not exonerate Earp or his confederates or make the decision any less a fraud.

Stuart N. Lake, Wyatt Earp's biographer gave a different version of the fight in his book "*Wyatt Earp: Frontier Marshal.*" Lake's research indicates that Earp was the scapegoat of an unsuccessful frame, attempted by Martin Julian, the owner of the San Francisco newspaper, who had bet $20,000 on Fitzsimmons. Wyatt Earp in the book writes again that he emerges spotlessly white, once again triumphant over evil. Most of the particulars in his highly probable account are missing, and therefore it is possible to accept Lake's research, that as referee Wyatt Earp called the fight as he saw it, regardless of the cost. Lake's version is mentioned here because of the emphasis which has been placed upon Earp's role in the affair, according to

Earp's memoirs and his conversations with Stuart Lake about the fight.

Without exception the contemporary accounts implicate Wyatt Earp, either as perpetrator or co-conspirator with Lynch or Julian. Of those involved in the fight, Wyatt Earp is always included among the conspirators. Yet there is evidence that the real reality is that Wyatt Earp was the scapegoat of a fix, if in fact it really was a fix. Such a synopsis would explain Earp's statement that he *"would talk later"* after the others had their say, and kept his usual silence during the affair until the hearing. Wyatt Earp was involved in a lot of skirmishes with the law over the years but kept his opinions to himself, and in all cases, he was cleared of any wrongdoing.

Wyatt Earp's situation was rather sharply described by Charles Asher a well known gambler of his time who was present at ringside during the match between Bob Fitzsimmons and Tom Sharkey on the night of December 2, 1896;

> *"Wyatt Earp will find it no easy matter to square himself with the sporting people. He may be perfectly innocent of any complicity in a scheme to rob Bob Fitzsimmons of the fight, but under the circumstances, he will have a hard job to clear his skirts of the odium that is being cast upon him."*

One has to wonder if Wyatt Earp's honesty will ever be cleared, and in all fairness, it must be added that the huge pile of evidence against Earp suggests the reason why.

After all the speculation is over a few observations of a more concrete nature can be made. The fix, again if it was a fix had little effect on the careers of the two fighters involved.

Fitzsimmons went on to defeat Sharkey in four rounds in 1899 and eventually became the Heavyweight Champion of the World. Tom "Sailor" Sharkey also went on to have a great boxing career but he was never crowned a champion at any weight level.

Although the Wyatt Earp fix scandal had little effect on the careers of Sharkey and Fitzsimmons, it finished boxing in California for many years to follow and the scandal destroyed the reputation of the National Athletic Club in San Francisco. Wyatt Earp's troubles in regards to this event did not seem concern him because the following year he and his wife Josephine Marcus Earp, departed for the gold fields in Alaska. After the gold rush ended in Alaska, they returned to California and most people had forgotten the night he almost knocked out boxing in California.

The author found the following article that was written by Barbara Allen in 1995. I think it sums up my thoughts completely regarding Wyatt Earp as a boxing referee;

When Referee Wyatt Earp Laid Down the Law

By Allen Barra
Published: November 26, 1995

> *All a man has got to show for his time here on earth is what kind of name he had. Now, Wyatt Earp, who would have told him when he was fighting crooks and standing up for his principles that there'd be a television show about him? That kids on the street would say, 'I'm Wyatt Earp. Reach.' "*

As a child and young adult the generation of baby boomers knew Earp as a somewhat earthier character, a part-time peace officer and full-time "sporting man" in Tombstone, Arizona. In fact, if Ali had been a contemporary of his idol, Jack Johnson, he might have known Earp not as the hero of the West's most famous gunfight but as the goat of a legendary prizefight held a century ago, on Dec. 2, 1896.

Wyatt Earp established his boxing credentials before he carried a gun. As a teen-ager he was a skillful boxer, but his real talent was as a referee. He was regarded highly enough by the rough-and-tumble rail splitters and buffalo hunters of the Wyoming railroad crews in 1868 to officiate while holding the fighters' purses and the betting money, no small double duty.

The gunfight at the O. K. Corral on Oct. 26, 1881, would eventually make Earp the most famous lawman in American history, even though he was never a full town marshal or county sheriff of Dodge City, Tombstone or anywhere else. But by 1882, Earp's career as a lawman was essentially over. For the remaining 47 years of his life, Wyatt Earp was to be a full-time sporting man.

From 1882 to 1894, Wyatt and Josephine Sarah Marcus, the actress from San Francisco he had met in Tombstone, lived throughout the West, gambling, prospecting and managing horses, and Wyatt occasionally officiating prizefights. The Earp's eventually settled in San Francisco and Wyatt had no trouble adapting to life there in the 1890's; a city directory from the period lists him as a "capitalist." The capital was a string of race horses.

San Francisco was also home to Gentleman Jim Corbett, the first heavyweight champion of the world to be crowned under Marquis of Queensberry rules. Thus, when Corbett retired temporarily in 1895, San Francisco was the natural stage for a title fight. The meeting pitted two of the best heavyweights in the world: the stocky native Irishman, Sailor Tom Sharkey, and Ruby Bob Fitzsimmons, a spindly legged, 170-pound former Australian blacksmith.

There was no problem dealing with the local police: Boxing was illegal, but very popular. The problem was finding a referee, as Sharkey's camp frustrated everyone by nixing several candidates. Desperate by the day of the fight, the prestigious National Athletic Club of San Francisco asked Earp if he would consider the job.

Earp wavered at first but then he accepted, reasoning that his arbitration of the fight might add gloss to his resume: "I don't know but what it will be a little bit of tone for me to referee a fight of this kind." What it gave him was a starring role in the first great controversy in American boxing history.

It began when Fitzsimmons's manager, Martin Julian, declared that Ruby Bob's corner refused Earp as referee. Exactly why is not clear, though it may have simply been because Sharkey's people said yes. Another possibility was Earp's inexperience with Marquis of Queensberry rules. Earp had officiated at London Prize Ring bouts, where mayhem from biting to eye-gouging was allowed.

Wyatt Earp offered to step down, but the National Athletic Club committee stuck by its choice, a decision that proved to be a minor flap compared with what happened when Earp stepped into the ring and a surprised police captain noticed he was carrying a gun. For the first time in boxing history, a local journalist later noted, "It became necessary to disarm the referee." Before the night was over, Earp would be wishing he had held onto the gun.

When the fight began, the taller, quicker Fitzsimmons dominated the slower Sharkey from the opening bell. In the eighth, Fitzsimmons struck with his famed "solar plexus punch," an uppercut under the heart that could render a man temporarily helpless. A year later that punch would put the newly un-retired Jim Corbett out and make Fitzsimmons the heavyweight champion, but the technique of flooring an opponent with a body blow was still new in 1896 and caught the crowd, Earp, and, indeed, Sharkey, by surprise.

Sharkey, clutching his groin and rolling on the canvas, screamed foul. Earp hurried over to examine him, and a few minutes later a stunned crowd saw the legendary former lawman climb through the ropes and head for the exits. It took a while for the buzz to circulate through the crowd of 10,000, most of whom had never seen a foul called in a boxing match, that Earp had awarded the victory to Sharkey.

Fitzsimmons versus Sharkey might have been the most anticipated fight yet held on American soil; some fans had paid the outrageous sum of $10 for seats, and now it had ended on a foul few had seen.

When Sharkey refused to be examined by the medical examiner for the National Athletic Club, a full-fledged scandal broke. Fitzsimmons fueled the fire by telling all who would listen that he was "simply robbed," while Earp was equally adamant that he had simply called it as he saw it. He even told a reporter for The Examiner that his friend, Bat Masterson, a fellow deputy from Dodge City who had gone to New York as a sportswriter, had lost money on the fight.

Fitzsimmons and his manager took court action against Sharkey and the National Athletic Club, but what was really on trial was Earp's reputation. The court's decision, rendered after two weeks of testimony, did nothing to dispel the increasing accusations that Earp and the Sharkey camp had conspired to fix the fight. The judge's ruling was that by engaging in a prizefight the combatants were "committing an offense against the law" and thus it was "not the sort of case for a court to consider." Many observers noted that the court took up nearly two weeks to come to that conclusion. At least Earp rendered his judgment quickly.

Though he never was the referee at a boxing match again, Earp continued to run with the sporting crowd. Less than a year after the Sharkey-Fitzsimmons fight, Earp and Masterson were hired as special policemen at the Fitzsimmons-Corbett fight in Reno, and Dempsey recalls Wyatt and Bat collecting weapons from the crowd at his fight with Jess Willard in Toledo, Ohio, in 1919. Earp remained a fight fan until his death in 1929.

Bob Fitzsimmons and Tom Sharkey went on to fight two more times with Fitz winning both bouts. They later became friends and joked about the controversy. But Earp never lived down his decision in the 1896 fight. At the time, and for the next couple of decades, opinion in the boxing world was split between a belief that Earp and Sharkey's corner had engineered a fix and that Earp, Sharkey and Fitzsimmons
were all in on it.

It's time to let Earp off the historical hook on both counts. There is no indication that Wyatt did anything but *make a tough call in a tough situation, as referees from Dave Barry (in the 1927 Dempsey-Tunney long count) and Richard Steele (in the 1990 Julio Cesar Chavez-Meldrick Taylor fight) were to do years later.*

What more than likely happened 100 years ago this Dec. 2 was that the O. K. Corral controversy of 15 years earlier finally caught up to Wyatt Earp. Interestingly, he went to his grave more famous for a decision in a fight that is now forgotten than for the shootout that has made him a household name today.

Below is a photo of Wyatt Earp as he looks out his back yard over the Colorado River. This photo was taken in 1928 one year before he passed away. This photo was found in our National Archives.

Chapter Eleven

Over this chapter the author would like to present an article that was published in the San Francisco Examiner newspaper on December 3, 1896. This author believes that Wyatt Earp should have the opportunity to defend himself.

"YES IT WAS A GREAT FIGHT BUT"

WYATT EARP.

That is just about as far as anybody Cares to Go in questioning Referee Wyatt Earp's Decision

Did Fitzsimmons hit Sharkey a foul blow? This is a question, which will be asked and debated for years to come whenever San Franciscans are gathered together. A quiet mild mannered man named Wyatt Earp says he did. He was the referee. His word goes. The purse and the bets go with it.

Anybody who wishes to dispute the matter with Mr Earp is invited to take the the job of my hands. For they do say down in Arizona that the swivel play with which he brings his battery into action is a marvel in gunnery, and when he negligently fans the trigger there are few who care to remain in the neighborhood and take lessons in ballistics.

He is something of a prototype of that "quite Mr. Brown, who on several occasions had cleaned out the town," so when Mr. Earp, referee on the occasion last evening when Robert Fitzsimmons and Thomas Sharkey fought with each other for $10,000 and all the honors of the prize ring, told in the eighth round that Mr. Fitzsimmons had struck Mr. Sharkey a low blow, and that consequently Mr. Sharkey had won the fight, no one cared to rise and say, "you're a perjured villain" or make any other remark indicating doubt or reproach. But once Mr. Earp had passed from view all sorts of people began saying all sorts of things, and they'll keep on saying them for many years to come.

And you ought to hear Mr. Fitzsimmons himself on that subject, and also Mr. Martin Julian, brother in law of the manager. They are doing enough talking for apolitical campaign and making statement which are quite rash enough for the angry aftermath of a presidential election. Surely they are entitled to talk for $10,000 is a lot of money to lose on one man's word, not to count the honor of victory and the sting of defeat. The referee's word goes, there is not getting behind those returns.

On the next page is a photo that was

published in this newspaper article.

EARP
REFEREE

Certainly there is no reason why Fitzsimmons should have stuck the foul blow. He had all the better of the fighting. He was himself strong on his legs and had a dal of driving power left in his arms. Without a foul he almost certainly would have won.

Those who cavil will say that Sharkey, himself a foul fighter, tricked the referee, having been taught by his experience just how to claim a foul. Then again before the fight, Martin Julian had said he had been informed that the referee had been "fixed!

But no one was running around last night to tell Mr. Earp those arguments. There was no wild rush at him to make the innuendoes. He was entirely free from those who bubbled over with suspicions. Somehow or other Mr. Earp was not remonstrated with. And he didn't have his gun.

That gun was in the inside pocked of Captain Whittman during all the exciting

141

period after the decision was rendered. The incident of the disarming was really an event of the evening. When Mr. Earp took the stage at the call of Billy Jordan, master of ceremonies, he was fortified on barbette.

Then Mr. Jordan made his remarks about having heard the referee was fixed. He didn't make these remarks personal. In fact he expressed the highest regard for Mr. Earp personally. He had heard these disquieting rumors, however, and consequently felt called upon to protest. He seemed to squint over apprehensively to where the Earp artillery might at any moment begin volleying and thundering. It would be a poor sort of a shot who would miss Martin Julian.

Billy Jordan, boxing promoter
1832 to 1916

"Have you got your gun?" asked Captain Whittman of Earp, noting Julian's uneasiness.

"Yep," was Wyatt Earp's remark "You'd better let me have it."

142

"All right."

Then Wyatt hands his pistol to Police Captain Whittman. So for the first time in the history of he ring in California, it was necessary to disarm the referee. Possibly if the surrender of the weapon had been more generally observed there would have been more willingness to debate with Mr. Earp over the correctness of his views about the foul.

Apart form the unsatisfactory ending, the fight was good enough for anybody's money. There was enough uncertainty to keep the nerves on edge. Most of the time it was anybody's fight, and the give and take was always fast and full of possibility.

Sharkey was as his friend had said was a hard man to hurt and an earnest fighter. Fitzsimmons fulfilled all expectations of being a great ring general and a hard puncher. Certainly his superiority as a boxer was manifest throughout the match.

BUT! That but ruined all the fun of the thing surrounding the fight. Men will never feel certain that the fight was on the square, and that the best man was not tricked out of it. They will continue to say that the referee was misled and Sharkey, faked the foul.

There were people enough for a national convention. They were not those of whom Fitz James O'Brien sang, "there faces beaten in by the iron hoof of sin." That may have been the sort of people who gathered at the ring side on the turf in O'Brien's day when "two young men busy and tall with nothing between them of strife or wrongs" got together to slug and swat and maul each other, "hammer and tongs."

But last nights company began with the man who passes the plate in church and ended with Justice of the Supreme Court. The clubs were crowded before the event. Many the man whose wife went to bed last night commiserating with him on the fact that he had to work so hard at the office. Many the lawyer who had to meet an important client. Many the leaders of the city's thoughts and action's, softened his conscience with tales of he necessity of ascertaining whether or not those boxing contests are really brutal.

Over in Oakland the good matrons came near to postponing a cotillion at the request of the dancing men. As it was, I fear many an Oakland belle experience all the woes of a wallflower at that cotillion, for there were Oakland dancing men in droves at the fight.

Police commissioners were there, and superior court judges, and their eyes danced at the sight of blood, and their breath came hard when the fortunes of battle swayed, for they are very human, the police commissioners and superior court judges. The produce exchange, the board of trade, the merchant's association, even the professionally good people of the civic federation were all representatives seemed a bit ashamed. For Theodore Roosevelt and Dr. Parkhurst have said that this ring fighting is not brutal and surely they should know.

Women were there, some with veils and some without. I don't suppose that even Mr. Roosevelt or Dr. Parkhurst would say that it was just the place for women. Certainly the men who howled and yelled about the ring didn't think so. Men don't care to hae women see them when they take the bit of morality in their teeth and let their passions run away with them.

Chinamen were there sitting in common brotherhood with the whites. That may be called a step into the direction of social equality, nd they ll yelled just the same.

There wasn't much yelling when the fight went on, but once or twice there rose that low, tense dangerous sound;

"Woo-on! Woo-on! Woo-On!"

That's the sound of the mob, the menace of the broiling human stream when it threatens to break the dam of order and roll on destroying. It greeted Julian when he protested the selection of Earp as referee. It rolled up against Sharkey every time he struck Fitzsimmons I tactics, which had proved so effective in the clinches or tried his wrestling tactics that proved so effective against Corbett.

Buy when the decision came there was no sign of riot. It took the crowd some time to ascertain just what had happened. Those who did know were not eager to mix things with Wyatt Earp, and the information came general by a slow trickling process, passing from mouth to mouth and tier to tier. So by the time the full significance of the situation had reached the throng, Earp had gone. Sharkey had been carried

Martin Julian 1869-1919

Sharkey had been carried away and there was no one left to mob but the police and Fitzsimmons, who left the ring protesting like one possessed.

Consequently it will be said that San Francisco accepted the decision gracefully, and the men who had staked fortunes on Earp's few fatal words won and lost their money with Christian fortitude and gentlemanly forbearance.

The money won and lost on Sharkey's staying power as honest money, no matter who may be bold enough to question the final results. Most bets had gone up that the stocky sailor would not last six or seven rounds. But up to the eighth he was there all the while.

At the end of the third, Fitzsimmons leaned over to those in his corner and said, "I'll finish him off in the next round." But Fitz did not finish off Sharkey. In fact at the end of the fourth it looked very much as though Sharkey could stay in the ring with the Australian a week or more.

In the fifth round it was different, Fitz got his arms into action and sharkey was battered more than he had ever been battered by the seas. But in the sixth he braced wonderfully and won the cheer which greeted him when the gong sounded that the sixth round money was all for the Sharkey man. Then in the seventh he kept fairly strong though few they were, who had any notion that he could possibly win anything more than the seventh round bets.

And then! Then cam a mix-up and a swirl of arms and Sharkey went down to claim foul. If the fight had ended with the seventh, few would have hd a twinge or regret. But as it is, Fitzsimmons has placed his case into the hands of Colonel Henry I. Kowalski in an effort to prevent the payment of the $10,000 check, which was the price for which they fought, and the big Australian's friends are crying in places where the quiet Mr. Earp will be certain not to hear them.

But it was a great occasion. If you don't think so, you should have seen Chief Crowley in his full uniform. He couldn't have done more had the President of the United States arrived. An you should have seen the crowd, which was fit to receive any president, even the "Advance Agent of Prosperity." You should have seen the fight.

Below is a drawing by the reporter at ringside that was published in the Salt Lake Herald newspaper on December 7th 1896.

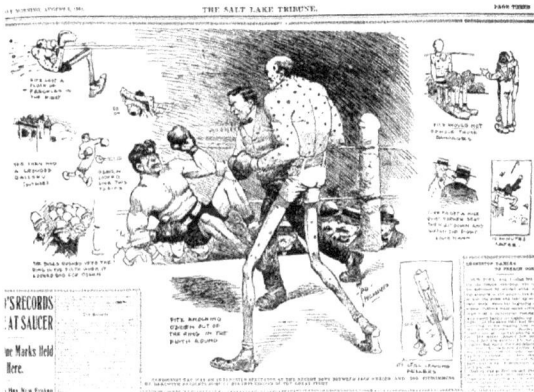

Summary

Even though some of the evidence presented shows that Wyatt Earp may have been involved in the fix, it must be noted that in his hearing, Earp testified, under oath that he had nothing to do with any fix. Again, Wyatt Earp lived on the line between right and wrong but he NEVER stepped over the line and for sure he never lied under oath. It must also be noted also that Wyatt Earp tried to decline on two separate occasions from taking the job of the referee of this major heavyweight championship fight. He declined the job when he first met the men in charge, and told them to get another man to referee.

Then a day before the boxing match the powers to be called him back for another interview, telling him they could not find a referee available and asked him again to consider taking the job. Earp stated in his memoirs and conversation with his biographer Stewart Lake and several other of his close friends that he took the job after they pleaded with him and that both fighters managers as well as Martin Julian, the promoter of the fight along with the staff of the National Athletic Club were all present and coerced Earp into taking the job.

As the author studied the research found on Wyatt Earp, and discovered that Earp drank coffee coffee was two-fold as a lawman, he needed every edge possible in dealing with law breakers. He told Bat Masterson;

"Drinking alcoholic beverages on this job is a bad mistake and if you do you will probably end-up dead. I know one thing for sure. Drinking liquid courage

149

leads to violence, and most men who drink do crazy things they would not normally do. I personally know that when I was drinking that I made some bad decisions. So if I don't drink, then I will surely make better decisions and I know that I will always have the upper hand on any man who does drink alcoholic beverages.

The other reason Earp did not drink was due to the fact that after his first wife died, he went on a drinking spree for a month or so, and in his drunken state, out of money, he begged a man for enough money to buy a drink. When the man turned him down but offered to by him a meal, Earp pistol whipped the man, stole his horse and rode to another town in Iowa. He was arrested their on the charge of stealing a horse, which was a capital offense in those days. His father, who was a lawyer, bailed him out of jail and told Wyatt that it was not a federal offense so you skip town, head west and never return to Iowa or you will be executed.

From that day forward, Wyatt Earp, never drank an alcoholic beverage, just coffee. He was a law abiding man. There is no question that he was on the line between legal and illegal for all of his life. This author has found nothing in all of my research of this amazing man indicating he committed no evil deeds and in fact, tried to avoid gunplay by his lightning quickness and regard for life.

He was an entrepreneur, a Republican, and Wyatt Earp always found ways to put himself and his brothers in position's to make a good living. To his dying day he denied any wrong doing with regard to his supposedly taking a bribe to throw the

Fitzsimmons vs Sharkey Championship fight or any other fight. He was a man who spent most of his life as a lawman and taking a bribe was against his principles

It is interesting though that Wyatt Earp's life was full of controversy and being the first referee in boxing history to call a fight because of a low blow again shows Earp was not afraid to call it the way he saw it, a personality trait that followed him his whole life. In presenting as many facts as possible with regard to whether Wyatt Earp took a bribe to throw this fight, it is this author's opinion, guilty or not, like so many other amazing situations he was in, controversy will follow Wyatt Earp forever in history. He was a man of firsts in so many events during his amazing lifetime. Wyatt Earp and his brothers were entrepreneur's and along with Doc Holliday, who came from a wealthy Georgia family of doctors, lawyers, dentists and pharmacists were members of the Republican party and this fact was one of the main reasons, why Wyatt Earp was such good friends of Doc Holliday.

Most of the Southwest in those days was Democratic, so the Earps and Holliday aligned themselves Republicans when they arrived in Arizona, that also at that time was 95 percent Democratic. Wyatt Earp, through a bad series of events learned that drinking alcoholic beverages put him in a position to make some bad judgment calls. In all of the towns where Wyatt Earp severed as a lawman, there is no doubt he put himself and his friends in a position to make money.

In all of those towns, the owners of the establishments wanted drinking, gambling and prostitution to continue 24 hours a day so they could make money hand over fist, they did not want killing and shooting because it was bad for business. Wyatt Earp and his friends were hired to keep the peace, "keep the peace." In all of these towns, Earp set himself and his friends up with a sweet deal to keep the peace. He set each town up with a law that it was illegal to carry firearms in the town limits, each violator would be arrested, jailed overnight, taken in front of a local judge, where they were fined $50, Earp or the arresting officer would receive $25 and the judge would keep $25. This method kept peace and augmented each officer's $100 a month pay of on the average.

Wyatt Earp was a master of pistol whipping violators and hauling them to jail, always asking them first if they saw the signs indicating they were suppose to check their pistols upon arrival. If they said no, they would simply give him their guns, if they got argumental or defiant, he would simply grab their guns and knock them out or knock them out with one punch, and drag them to the jail. Wyatt Earp was an amazing athlete. He was 6'0 in heighth and weighed 190 lbs and had a fast and heavy punch.

He always wore a duster and kept a pistol in the pocket of the duster not in a holster. His badge was on his vest under the duster. When making his rounds he would simply walk up to men toting pistols, move right next to them, order a cup of coffee and make small talk, then he would ask them if they saw the signs and would take it from there.

He was afraid of no man, he knew that most men had liquid courage under their belt but he was sober and always had the upper hand because a man who was drinking has liquid courage but he knew he was quicker and proved it his whole life.

According to Bat Masterson, Earp was simply an amazing athlete. Doc Holliday practiced six hours a day, everyday with his guns and his throwing knives but Masterson wrote in his memoirs that Wyatt Earp never practiced shooting with his pistol but one evening as they were making the rounds together in Dodge City, Masterson wrote that a man came running out of a saloon with his guns blazing and as he turned the corner of the building, Earp drew his pistol and shot the running man in the butt just as he turned his butt toward them. Masterson said it was the most incredible shot he had ever seen. Earp did not want to kill the man just stop him and ask questions later. Bat Masterson said of Wyatt Earp that he was the most fearless man he had ever known.

ACKNOWLEDGEMENTS

Wyatt Earp: Frontier Marshal- By Stewart Lake, published in 1931

I Married Wyatt Earp- By Josephine Marcus Earp, published in 1976

Helldorado: Bringing the Law to Mesquite- By Billy Breakenridge, published in 1929

Bat Masterson: The Man and the Legend- By Robert K. DeArment, published in 1989

The Third Man- By Joseph Roemer- True Western Magazine- published in February 1957

The Night Wyatt Earp Almost KOed Boxing- by Gary Roberts- The West Magazine- published in November 1971

All "Fitz" – The Detroit Daily News- Article published on December 2, 1896

It's a Cinch-The Detroit Daily News- Article published on December 2, 1896

Sharkey Won on Foul- The Massillon Ohio Independent Newspaper, article published on December 7, 1896

Fitzsimmons Robbed- The San Francisco Examiner, published on December 8, 1896

Fight Dispute-The New York Times newspaper, article published on December 5, 1896

Fight Fixed- The New York Times newspaper, article published on December 10, 1896

Sharkey Cashes Check- The New York newspaper, article published on December 18, 1896

154

Wyatt Earp surrendering his gun- Drawing, article published in the San Francisco Examiner on December 4, 1896

Doctors at Tom Sharkey's bedside- Drawing, published in the San Francisco Examiner on December 7, 1896

A copy of the original signed $10,000 check, the San Francisco Examiner, article published on December 3, 1896

The Cartoon of Wyatt Earp, Holding a gun on Fitzsimmons, article published in the New York Times newspaper, published on December 4, 1896

Wikipedia Online Encyclopedia, Biography's of Bob Fitzsimmons, Tom Sharkey, Wyatt Earp and Bat Masterson.

When Referee Wyatt Earp Laid Down the Law, by Allen Barra, published article on November 26. 1995.

The Golden Age of Boxing, by Zeke Crandall, published in 2017

Yes It Was a Great Fight But- Published by the San Francisco Examiner, San Francisco, CA on December 4, 1896

About the Author

William "Tom" Vyles aka Zeke Crandall was born in London, Ontario, Canada. The family moved to Phoenix, Arizona in 1956. A life long battle with Asthma, several bouts with pneumonia, in an out of hospitals the first nine years of life, the family was instructed by physicians to move to Arizona for the hot dry climate.

In and out of school until age ten, home schooled by his mother Elizabeth, reading "The Books of Knowledge," encyclopedia, Tom fell in love with history. With no family in Arizona, our family adopted elderly neighbors, Kenny and Mary Harris, as our Arizona grandparents.

Kenny worked in the stockyards in Cincinnati as a brand inspector for cattle coming from Arizona. He became friends of John Wayne, who brought his cattle through the stockyards in Cincinnati. John talked Kenny into moving to Arizona. Kenny was a professional fiddle player, along with his friend Rudy MacDonald, who played banjo, they toured Arizona playing gigs.

Young Tom went along on most of the out of town music gigs. His job was to set up instruments and equipment. The carrot for Tom was that Kenny would take me rabbit and quail hunting the next day. Young Tom fell in love with Arizona history, because Kenny introduced him to many amazing older men, who told him stories of the old west.

This author's other 10 published books are available at my website, www.arizonatales.com, FB Tom Vyles, Amazon, or email zekecrandall46@hotmail

www.ingramcontent.com/pod-product-compliance
Lightning Source LLC
Chambersburg PA
CBHW060349090426
42734CB00011B/2081